Rift To Reunion

BOOKS CLINIC PUBLISHING

Published by Booksclinic Publishing
Empowering Authors, Inspiring Readers
Booksclinic Publishing
Bilaspur, Chhattisgarh, India
Website: www.booksclinic.com
Email: booksclinicpublishing@gmail.com

SKU Code:2732
ISBN: 978-93-7254-438-1
Edition Details:
First Edition: February,2026
Genre: Fiction story
Price: Rs. 199/- / $ 9

Credits
Cover Design: Aashish Dhuri
Interior Design: Asmi Awasthi

Publisher's Note

Booksclinic Publishing is dedicated to empowering authors and connecting them with over 20 lakh readers globally. The opinions and ideas expressed in this book are those of the author and do not necessarily reflect the views of the publisher.

For permissions, bulk orders, or author inquiries, please contact:
Email: booksclinicpublishing@gmail.com | **Phone: +9196910 66997**

Discover more inspiring stories at www.booksclinic.com

Printed in India

Dedication

My creative journey had long been rooted in poetry, drama, and essays. My wife, Sushila, along with our daughter Divya and son Varun Nagarajan, gently yet persistently awakened my deep interest in storytelling. Their unwavering belief in my potential inspired this foray into fiction. I dedicate this book to them, with love and gratitude.

I also would like to " Thank" my relative Miss Alagu Lakshmi and my neighbor Ms Devika for helping translate my Tamil version of Golden book award winner book " **Purithal Pothum**" to English.

Nagarajan
Dubai
21 January 2026

Foreword

First and foremost—dear reader— A few words about Nagarajan...

To understand him is to truly appreciate the depth of his character. Nagarajan, the creator of this work, has been a dear friend of mine for over thirty years. Professionally, he has served in senior roles within renowned companies across the globe. Yet, beyond the corporate sphere lies a heart driven by an insatiable artistic spirit.

That passion for the arts has led him to contribute actively to Tamil Sangam and cultural organisations in many countries. Wherever he has lived, he has left an indelible mark, consistently expressing his thoughts through poetry, essays, and plays.

He turned out to be a storyteller. However, it came as a surprise, even to someone familiar with his earlier creative pursuits. Upon reading this story, I was deeply moved.

Now, let us turn to the story itself.

His narrative is both engaging and skilfully crafted. From the very first page, it captures the reader's attention and holds it with quiet power.

Addressing a contemporary issue with clarity and emotional depth, the story resonates universally, inviting every reader to pause and reflect.

The story " Rift to Reunion " presents a clear and powerful resolution that vividly unfolds before the reader's eyes. It poignantly explores how the human mind can inflate a minor rift in a relationship into a significant divide—and at the same time, how that very mind, when viewed from a different perspective, can weave the strands back together. This paradox is nothing short of fascinating.

The author deftly addresses a common yet crucial issue faced by today's younger generation—the ambiguity and lack of clarity that often shroud the marital bond. With remarkable lucidity, the narrative brings this theme to light and leads us towards a strong, yet practical and constructive conclusion.

The central idea is masterfully underscored by the author through the concept that *"gain and loss in a marital relationship must be navigated with mutual understanding and cooperation."*

The story also raises a subtle yet powerful question: Can the modern woman, who breathes the air of freedom and embraces bold thinking, truly find happiness through those very choices? The final scene is simply extraordinary—it transforms harsh words into tender ones, as if rebirthing them through the emotional and soulful union of two beings.

Throughout the narrative, one finds a seamless blend of simplicity in style, elegance in storytelling, and a quiet undercurrent of philosophical insight. In one moment, the character says, "Ashok Nagar," prompting the thought—should he have said, "I'm from Ashok Nagar?" This small nuance beautifully captures the contrast between what is said and what is meant, revealing the inner facets of the mind with finesse.

This depth of reflection—where *"what matters is not the actions, but the intentions behind them,"* and the realisation that *"a generation must bow to rise again"*—is a mark of true literary craftsmanship. Such delicate streams of consciousness, layered with meaning, are the hallmark of a thoughtful writer. The author excels in this profound skill.

A humble request, dear friend— Among your multiple identities, it is the one as a storyteller that stands out as the most profound. This story not only affirms that truth, it stamps it with strength and clarity.

May your creative journey continue to flourish. May your stories bloom one after another, touching minds and hearts alike.

For readers, this story is sure to be a delightful and enriching experience.

Thank you…

With sincere appreciation,

Mathurai Veeran

Kotturpuram

Chennai – 600085

Message of Felicitation

It is with pride and affection that I write this foreword to the story From **Rift-to-Re-Union** penned by my dear cousin and storyteller, Mr Nagarajan.

Those who know him personally will agree that wherever he is, the atmosphere is always lively. He can deliver ten jokes in five minutes, effortlessly keeping a crowd entertained. So, when I was asked to write the foreword to his story, I expected a comic narrative. But to my surprise, he has written a tender, emotionally resonant love story that delicately connects with the intensity of the human heart.

With the very title ***Rift to Reunion***, he boldly introduces the central theme even before the narrative begins. This marks his courageous way of building a story, stating with absolute clarity that understanding is the foundation of all relationships. What follows is a moving tale of an emotional tug-of-war between two hearts. The situations depicted in this story feel so familiar—almost as though they are happening in the house next door. The realism is striking. Surely, we've all experienced the incidents described at least once.

It is impossible for two hearts to always think alike or act in perfect unison. Each mind has its nature and rhythm. When differences arise, they must be addressed and resolved through open conversation. But often, ego stands in the way. Instead of saying "you and I," people begin to say "you versus me," and the gap widens until they declare, "I don't need you anymore." In this digital era, even a missed phone call can spark misunderstanding. Spouses, friends, even family members drift apart over small things like unanswered calls. The author poignantly reminds us that love, marriage, and family life all require one essential thing: understanding. Every separation stems from a lack of it, and the solution lies in its presence. Hence, the title drafts as *Understanding is Enough.*

The protagonists, Rahul and Swetha, are true reflections of today's young couples. You don't just find them in this book—you'll find them all around you, in every neighborhood. Here are some lines from the story that particularly stayed with me:

1. *Any household where women can live without fear and with joy will flourish.*
2. *Suffering begins when we are unable to say "No" even when we know we should.*
3. *Those who cry "freedom" in everything may build their married lives with clay, trying to hold it within the iron frame of tradition.*
4. *With too much love, even a dog can become human—and equally, vice versa a human can become a dog.*
5. *No one can agree 100% with another person at all times.*

These observations are not just powerful—they are painfully true. Today, many marriages have become solely about earning money after the wedding. Even having children is seen as a burden, and raising them feels like an obligation. There is little thought about what family life truly means. This story reminds us that *family life*, too, is a kind of *virtue.* And to understand the truth, young people today *must* read this story.

With gratitude,
Kalyan Anand
Barani Street
Velachery
Chennai – 600042

Foreword

I've known Mr. Nagarajan ever since my family moved in next door to him and his wife, Mrs. Sushila. From the very beginning, what stood out to us was the ease and joy with which they shared their lives. Their companionship, rooted in travel and shared routines, was not something they spoke about, but something they quietly lived every day. It was hard not to notice, and even harder not to admire.

So, when Nagarajan mentioned that he was writing a book on marital relationships, it felt almost inevitable. He writes from a place of lived experience; well read, well travelled, and more importantly, well lived.

The original Tamil version was something I couldn't fully read, but having heard portions from him, I was struck by how naturally and almost poetically the narrative flowed. The story unfolds with honesty and simplicity, drawing you in without effort. I'm glad to have played a small role in bringing this English version of the book to life.

As someone who is fairly newly married myself, I found much of the book deeply relatable. It speaks gently yet truthfully about the small misunderstandings that, if left unattended, can grow into lasting wounds. It explores the quiet tensions many couples navigate today, the balance between independence and togetherness, between holding on to one's beliefs and making space for love. The book doesn't offer loud declarations or rigid answers; instead, it invites reflection. Through its attention to detail and emotional nuance, it nudges the reader to revisit their own words, actions, and silences, and perhaps imagine how things could be done a little differently.

I thank him for this opportunity and wish him many more Golden Book Awards as "Purithal Pothum" so deservedly received in Tamil.

Ms.Devika Nambiar
Chennai – 600056

Rift to Reunion

Rahul's admission into IIT Bombay marked a moment of immense pride for his family. Coming from a modest, middle-class background, this achievement stood as a testament to his relentless dedication and perseverance. His parents, Kamala and Krish, were overjoyed—truly *on cloud nine*—as they celebrated the outcome of their son's consistent hard work and many sleepless nights. Securing a place in one of the country's most prestigious institutions was a milestone, not just for Rahul but for the entire family.

Though the joy was immense, there lingered a practical concern. A seat at IIT Madras would have significantly reduced their financial burden. However, considering Rahul's excellent marks and the specific course he had chosen, the Mumbai campus emerged as the ideal fit. With a deep sense of faith, they left the final decision to fate, trusting that the Almighty had charted the best course for their son. Amid the preparations, Krish voiced his concerns to Kamala:

"When are we supposed to leave? How much are we expected to spend?" Worry clouded his thoughts as he considered the expenses related to Rahul's education and living costs. Kamala, grounded in practical realities, felt that merely discussing the financial pressure would not bring a solution, especially as she had limited influence outside her domestic responsibilities. She suggested seeking guidance from Krish's co-brother, Ananth Narayanan, whose son Siddharth had already graduated from IIT. However, Kamala hesitated. She was well aware of Ananth's tendency to exaggerate, and she felt it might not be wise to rely on him for accurate information. Instead, she considered asking Rahul's friends to help them estimate the average expenses involved in studying and living in Mumbai, the Commercial Capital of India.

At the same time, she was increasingly resentful of Krish's unemployment, especially since he had resigned from his previous job, citing issues at the workplace—something Kamala viewed more as an excuse than a necessity. As her thoughts raced, Rahul returned from a temple visit. Kamala, noticing him from the kitchen, momentarily forgot her worries. She admired him silently, his appearance reminded her of her father. Yet, she was struck by the irony that her father's intelligence, which had skipped a generation, now seemed to live on in Rahul.

To her, it represented an unusual but hopeful pattern in generational inheritance. Kamala carried within her a quiet dream that Rahul would uplift the family and change their circumstances. Yet, she remained deeply concerned about the future of her two daughters, whose marriage and security were still uncertain. Unlike Kamala, Krish was not burdened by such long-term worries. He tended to avoid anxiety, preferring silence over speculation.

Looking at Rahul, he asked calmly, "When do we leave for Mumbai?" "13th of next month," Rahul replied. The train tickets had been booked for the

13th, on the Dadar Express. As the departure approached, the reality of separation and financial strain began to weigh heavily. On the night of the 12th, Kamala remained sleepless, her mind consumed with both hope and concern for the journey ahead. "This child, who does not know Hindi, the language most of the people speak in Mumbai, wondering how he will study in that lively metro city without understanding the language fully.

Everything must go smoothly. She prays daily to her favorite God Lord Murugan. Krish is worried about how much money he can give him to send him off. On the evening of the 13th, everyone went to the Chennai Central station. The entire compartment was crowded. There were more people outside who had come to see off the travelers than those travelling by train, creating a mix of joy and sorrow.

The current scenes are A family is sending their daughter off after her wedding to her husband's family. A young husband is sending his wife to his in-law's house in Mumbai for childbirth. No matter how many times one says it is the same compartment, an elderly man struggles with doubt, wondering if he can check the ticket chart used to be pasted outside the compartment of the train. The young couple were bidding farewell to the old man, who was returning to the senior citizen comfort living home after staying for three weeks with his grandchildren.

The kids were wondering why their grandfather was leaving when they had a wonderful house and facilities in Chennai. The Mumbai Dadar (Chennai Express) departed majestically, carrying all the passengers.

At IIT Powai Orientation campus:
All the students have arrived, accompanied by their parents or relatives, such as brothers or uncles. Rahul, however, is alone. Everyone present is conversing in English or Hindi with an accent. Two individuals nearby were engaged in conversation. One of them appears to be a student who has been trained in Kota, Rajasthan, and has secured a place at IIT Mumbai.Kota, the Education Society of India. No one who was taught there, has faced failure. Regardless of the higher education path—be it medicine, engineering, or chartered accountancy—Kota Rajasthan is the best destination for training in India. The coaching centers in Kota are a testament to hard

work.Success is assured if one goes there. The student standing few yards away continued to converse with

the person nearby. Hearing all this, Rahul recalled the coaching centers in Rasipuram, Namakkal district, where he had been trained. In Tamil Nadu India, Namakkal district is indeed an educational hub, and it is quite similar there as well. It is all about studying, studying, and studying. The ability of these coaching centers is evident in their capacity to elevate students from scoring 95 marks to achieving 99.5 marks. Rahul felt that he should go and explain all of this to them.

However, there was a slight hesitation in his mind. How could he approach people he did not know? He remained silent. With no other option, he distanced himself from there. A person who approached Rahul asked in Hindi,

"Aur kitna time lagegaa ?"

"How much time will it take?"

Rahul understood a bit.
Was he asking when it would start?
Or when would it end?
Or how much longer does he have to wait here?
There was a slight confusion. he could barely understand Hindi. "No idea, sir," he replied, "I am also waiting." He glanced back at him.
Behind him, the young girl who was standing lightly tilted her head and seemed to be asking something to another girl who was behind her.

Her face was not visible. However, the place smelled of her perfume. She must be the daughter of the person standing next to him. After all formalities were completed, Rahul received his hostel room number and arrived at his room by 8:00 PM. He had to attend classes, early morning the following day.

In the morning, he quickly got up, had a good shower thinking of the whole day ahead. He was in the class room by 8 AM. As soon as he entered the classroom, he was tensed slightly. The students there were not like those he had seen at the Ashok Nagar school in Chennai where he completed his schooling. He sensed an inferiority complex within himself though the classes concluded smoothly the first day, with not much studying involved.

At home in Chennai, normally during lunchtime, after finishing his meal, his mother would serve him a small cup of coffee. Sipping that was a unique pleasure. With the thought of enjoying coffee, he walked towards the coffee counter located in the canteen. Achuthan Nair, person from the state of

Kerala, who had been working in the canteen for 30 years, approached him and asked,
"Tea or coffee?"
Rahul inquired about the price of the coffee as usual in his language Tamil. It felt strange...
Oh no, am I speaking in Tamil?
This guy may not understand.
He then asked, "How much is the coffee?" in English.
"Pachaas Rupiah" replied Achuthan Nair in Hindi. There was a slight confusion between 25 and 50 for Rahul.
Does Pachaas means 25 or 50? he was confused.
He opened his wallet and found a ₹100 note. He handed it over to him, saying, "I don't have change."
At that moment, that young girl whom he had seen the previous day walked towards the shop. She spoke fluently in both Hindi and Malayalam languages to the man.

The girl said, "Mere ko ek de do... usko ek de do." The man extended two cups towards her and she said, "Uncle... coffee is a bit hot... please give me an empty cup." in Hindi.

Rahul was surprised at how she could speak English, Hindi, and Malayalam so effortlessly. For people who lived in south or in Chennai Tamilnadu, apart from Tamil, everything else seems to be a struggle he thought.

It was the first time he saw her standing close by. She was a petite girl with sharp eyes, and thick hair. There was a small dot between her two eyebrows. She wore blue jeans and a yellow top, as if it had been tailored just for her. For Rahul, Memories of his classmates from the twelfth grade in Chennai and some young women he had seen near Ashok Nagar in Chennai came to his mind. In the school he attended, they followed very strict rules. All the girls would come to school with their hair tied up and in school uniforms. But the girl in front of him was different. There is something special in her that made him to look at her again. She offered him the cup of coffee. After a moment of hesitation, he took the cup. The coffee cup wobbled slightly.

Slowly, their friendship began without any further hesitation.

She came next to him and extended her hand, saying, "Hi, I am Swetha." He replied, "I am Rahul." They both drank their coffee in silence and then She asked,

"I am from Pune, what about you?"

He responded, "I am from Chennai."

"Oh, are you a Tamilian ?" she inquired in Tamil language.

He was taken aback.

He never expected her to speak in Tamil. A sense of joy welled up inside him. He smiled gently at her. There were no traces of Tamil culture in her. Initially, he thought she might be from Gujarat or Maharashtra.

He contemplated whether to speak in Tamil or not. She then resumed speaking in English, asking in English about his home in Chennai. He replied 'Ashok

Nagar'. He thought, he should have told that I am from Ashok Nagar. She then continued..
"My grandfather and grandmother are from Madurai My father is settled here in Pune " We used to go to Madurai during our summer holidays. For Rahul, the way she spoke Tamil language gave him a pleasant surprise.
Rahul said " Bye" and she asked
" Why are you in a hurry ?"

He had to prepare for the next day to attend the first session on cybersecurity. In Ashok Nagar school, it was enough to just carry a bag. However, in IIT, one needs to study extensively to pay attention in class and ask meaningful questions.

First day in the class room. When listening to the Professor, Rahul was not able to concentrate. His mind was searching for whether Swetha had arrived. She had been sitting right behind him. How was it possible, he wondered, that even when our eyes face forward, we can still feel the presence of the people we hold closest, even when they stand somewhere behind us?

It was as if the heart had its own secret vision, a soft intuition that never quite fades. Maybe that was what people meant by the mind's eye—that invisible thread that keeps us connected, even in silence. It has been a week since then.

It was Saturday the next day and everyone had various assignments. They were discussing how to proceed.

Rahul remained quietly seated at one end. Swetha came next to him and asked, "Can I join you?"
He replied, "Please do."
The friendship continued. It became the norm for the two of them to come together, sit side by side, and frequently discuss the project. Everyone had noticed it—the glances, the easy way they moved around each other—and soon the whispers began. Soft little comments, shared behind hands and in crowded hallways, about what a perfect pair they would make. It was impossible not to hear it; the murmurs seemed to float in the air around them, as though the whole world had an opinion. For six long months, he had lived with an unspoken stress of his own.

Each day brought him a little closer to the decision, and now, with Diwali Festival only a week away, time felt suddenly more precious, edged with expectation. And then, almost without thinking, he said it. That he would be going to his hometown Chennai for Diwali. The words came softly, slipping into the quiet moment while Swetha was still talking, her voice warm and steady beside him. Yet everything seemed to pause around his confession.

There was something in the way he said it—something tender, tentative, hopeful—that made her hold her breath. As if this simple announcement carried a world of meaning, waiting to unfold. She responded, "Very nice." She added, "Your parents and sisters must be waiting for you." I will be taking the train to Chennai for Diwali, specifically the Dadar Express.

The same house… the same mother and father… the same sisters he had known all his life. Yet, without meaning to, his mind kept drifting back to Swetha, comparing her to them in quiet, unguarded moments. It unsettled him sometimes—the way a single person could slip so easily into the fabric of his thoughts.

Even in the smallest things, Swetha appeared. When his sisters, Uma and Meena, came close to speak to him, he found himself noticing details he had never cared about before. Their eyebrows… untouched, unshaped, left exactly as they had always been. Swetha, on the other hand, shaped hers with such care, such effortless grace, as though beauty were simply a part of her nature.

He questioned himself in those private moments.

Why didn't his sisters ever bother?

Why was he even thinking about such things?

But the truth lingered, gentle and undeniable—Swetha had changed something in him, awakened a softness he had not known was there. And now, even the familiar felt strange, touched by the quiet shadow of her presence in his thoughts.

He wondered.

On the morning of " Diwali festival" , his mother came next to him after having the traditional oil bath. Though the fragrance of wood pressed oil was in the air, all Rahul could recall was the fragrance of Swetha's shampoo and her daily-use perfume lingering at the tip of his nose.

Is this what love is?

No... no... it can't be, he told himself.

Diwali ended, and Rahul was back in his college hostel in Mumbai.

In those five days when he was in Chennai not a single call or even a WhatsApp message came from Swetha. He wondered whether he should have messaged her at least once. Just as he stepped into the classroom, he saw Swetha walking towards him from a distance. His heart began to race.

As she came closer, he said, “Hi.”

She looked at him and said, “I missed you.”

I missed you too," he wanted to say, but the words felt too simple for the complex emotions swirling within him. Rahul wanted to tell her how much her voice meant to him, how countless memories of her came to him when he was in Chennai.

Rahul wanted to tell her that she was more than just someone he missed; He wanted to tell her that he felt as if she was an essential part of his world. He wanted to tell her that he was complete when she was near, that her simple words had the power to mend the cracks in his soul. He wanted to tell her that he had missed her not just with his mind, but with every fiber of his being.

Sometimes, the courage that women possess is something that men don't. Rahul was not able to communicate what he wanted to… College had resumed after the holidays, but there wasn't much academic pressure yet.

After the classes, while coming out, "This evening, I've booked a Shah Rukh Khan film at a mall in Andheri. I have two tickets.

Would you like to join?" she asked.

"My friend Shirin was supposed to join, but she had some last-minute work. That's why I have an extra ticket," she explained. For Rahul, Hindi films weren't his choice. But when going with Swetha, *any* movie seemed enjoyable—his heart whispered so. "Alright, I'll come," Rahul replied. "Just meet me directly at the theatre. I'll see you there," Swetha said. There was no special corner seat like they show in the movies, just two seats in the middle of the row they got. Still, his mind couldn't focus on the movie. His thoughts kept drifting to Swetha, who was seated beside him. Once the movie ended, they were leaving the movie hall, Swetha said

"Come, let's grab a bite before heading back," They stepped into a nearby Chinese restaurant. As soon as they sat down, she asked softly,

"What would you like to have?" He had been to countless Chinese restaurants before, yet in that moment, not a single dish came to his mind.

"**Anything**," he said with a shy smile.

"There's no dish called ***'Anything'***," she replied, her eyes sparkling.

When she smiled, he couldn't help but notice her flawless teeth—spotless, perfectly aligned pearls. A tiny dimple appeared on her right cheek, and he felt he could gaze at her forever. "

Whatever you order," he said gently, "I'll have the same." And so, they shared their meal and stepped out together—two hearts lighter than they had been when they walked in. They booked an Uber for the ride back. It was decided—she would drop him off first before heading home.

Somewhere in Rahul's mind, a quiet unease began to stir.
A man's **ego** What was this?
Everything he believed he should be doing, she had already done—booking the movie tickets, choosing the restaurant, placing the order, paying the bill, calling the cab, and even making sure he was dropped off first. Was she taking over what he was meant to do? he wondered.

And yet, beneath that flicker of discomfort, something softer bloomed. A gentle joy. Their dinners together… their movie nights… the shared laughter—all of it had become a beautiful habit. If they didn't see each other even for a day, something felt incomplete.

The next Monday evening.

As they stepped out of class, classmates Arpan Srivastava and Apoorva Pandey walked up to Swetha and Rahul, holding a box of sweets in their hands. Apoorva turned to Swetha and said,

"Arpan and I are in love. Our families have agreed. The engagement is on this Sunday at Lonavala. You must come!" she beamed.

"Exactly what everyone expected"

Swetha smiled. She had been observing them for months and had always guessed this day would come. Looking at Rahul, Swetha said,

"You should come along! " Swetha and Apoorva were close friends. But Rahul didn't share such a bond with Arpan. Still… a trip to Lonavala with Swetha? Though his mind hesitated, his head nodded "yes" on its own. If the function is on Sunday, they had to leave by Saturday evening. Lonavala was very close to Pune, and Swetha had visited the place several times. It was nothing new to her.

But for Rahul, it would be his first time. All he knew was that Lonavala, like Ooty or Kodaikanal in Tamilnadu, was a hill station.
How do we go? By train?
Or should we rent a car?
What gift are we taking?
How much will it all cost?
His mind had already begun calculating.
But a part of his brain asked: *No matter the cost, I should make it* Will an opportunity like this ever come again? Swetha herself is asking me to join her. Why would I overthink it?
On Friday morning, Swetha called. "I've booked Tatkal train tickets for both of us," she said. Tatkal, which literally means "immediate" in Hindi, is a program by Indian Railways in which you can book train tickets almost on time for urgent travel plans.

Rahul was happy and he was thinking there is no "Tatkal" concept in getting close to someone whom you like. Swetha called the previous day and asked whether Rahul is ready and packed his things ?

Ready …"Or are you like me

packing your bag and getting ready only at the last minute?" she teased.

"No, I'm ready," he replied. Truthfully, he hadn't prepared anything.

But, when Swetha asked, that was the only answer he could give. Since she had been the one to book their tickets, he had imagined—perhaps even hoped—that their seats would be side by side. It felt natural, almost destined.

But when her message arrived, the soft ping of WhatsApp echoing in the quiet of his room, reality settled differently.

Her seat: **B-59.** His seat: **B-69.**

Ten numbers apart. Ten small spaces that suddenly felt like an ocean.

A faint, unexpected ache stirred inside him. It was foolish, he told himself. Illogical. And yet the feeling lingered, stubborn and tender.

Who is she to me? he wondered.

Why should it matter where she sits?

They were simply classmates—same university, same course, a shared language that made conversations easy. No promises. No definitions. Nothing that could reasonably explain the heaviness he felt.

And yet… there it was. That quiet, undeniable pull he couldn't name. Saturday morning, 6 a.m.

The city was still stretching awake when they arrived at the old station—V.T. Station, now proudly renamed Chhatrapati Shivaji Terminus. Beneath its towering arches, the world felt grand, almost cinematic. The train they were meant to board, Train number **11007**, waited on platform two, humming with the promise of departure. Their classmates had gathered too, a small crowd of familiar faces, laughter, and luggage. And by some gentle stroke of fate, all of them had been placed in the same compartment—close enough for conversations, but still not close enough for him. Until Swetha's close friend Madhavi spoke.

She stood with the ease of someone who noticed what others tried to hide. Smiling, she offered him her seat **B-60** choosing instead to take his place.

It was a simple gesture, nothing dramatic in the eyes of the world. But to him, it felt like the universe had quietly shifted. As he thanked her, something warm bloomed in his chest—a joy so sudden, so unguarded, it startled him.

A joy that had everything to do with one person sitting just one seat away. And in that single moment, he knew—somewhere deep, somewhere still unnamed—that his feelings for her were no longer something he could ignore. Rahul felt an inexplicable joy. It was only a few hours' journey, yet the very thought of sitting beside Swetha, chatting and spending that time with her, brought immense happiness. He didn't show it outwardly, but deep inside, he felt a quiet contentment.

Just five minutes before departure, a Gujarati family boarded the train in a hurry—a senior gentleman, his wife, and a little girl, possibly their granddaughter, around eight years old. The elderly man came straight to Rahul and asked,

"Can I take your window seat?

The little one wants to sit there." spoke in Hindi language.

Though Rahul couldn't follow Hindi entirely, he understood that the man was requesting his seat. Only a few moments ago, Rahul had felt lucky to be seated beside Swetha.

Now, this unexpected dilemma. His heart said no, but his head nodded in agreement.

"No… It's a bit difficult.

I need the power connection to work on my laptop. The plug point is on this side," he tried to avoid giving away the seat. Noticing the conversation, Swetha said, "It's alright. You can take my seat. I don't mind moving." To Rahul, that offer felt even worse.

But, fortunately, the little girl said, "I don't want that seat. I'll sit here," and settled into her seat.

"Phew… Thank God," Rahul murmured under his breath. Swetha looked at him and asked,

"What are you muttering?" "Nothing…" he replied. The train departed to Lonavala on time. For the first time, Swetha allowed Rahul to step softly into the fragile corners of her past. Her voice held a shy music as she spoke of her childhood, of the girl she had once been.

She told him how, back in Class 10, a boy named Arjun had slipped her a love letter—an earnest, trembling confession written in hurried schoolboy handwriting. And how she, frightened and innocent, had carried it straight to her father and placed it in his hands. Rahul had never laid eyes on Arjun, yet he felt a strange, unexpected tightness in his chest—an irrational flicker of jealousy toward a boy who existed only in Swetha's memory. She turned to him then, her head tilted just slightly, her eyes warm with curiosity.

"Tell me,"she asked softly,

"did you ever give someone a love letter?

Or receive one?"

The question brushed gently against places he rarely visited. In truth, Rahul had never received a love letter. And he had never found the courage to offer one. The only message that had ever come close was a single text—Hi, you are so cute...—a message he later discovered had been meant for his friend Bharath, not for him.

How could he possibly tell her that? His thoughts drifted suddenly to his friend Kumar from Ashok Nagar. Kumar's sister had once rejected a perfectly respectable groom—well-earning, well-mannered, employed in a top IT company in Chennai— simply because he had never been in a relationship. "I can't marry someone whom no one ever loved," his friend's sister had said firmly.

Times had changed. Today's young women think differently. Once, a man was expected to love no one until after marriage; even the rumor of a past affection had been enough to cloud his reputation.

Purity had been defined in strange, narrow ways. But now... the world had softened, opened. Friendships, heartbreaks, quiet confessions, the bittersweet ache of first love—none of it was shameful anymore.

It was seen almost as a kind of gentle credential, proof that one had lived and felt. All these thoughts swirled through Rahul's mind as he looked at Swetha. She was waiting, eyes bright, lips curved in a teasing smile.

He felt his own smile rise—awkward, tender, helpless. "Okay, okay," she laughed lightly, "don't be embarrassed." And in that moment, something warm and quietly hopeful settled between them. You don't have to say anything," she said gently. Rahul was surprised at Swetha's honesty. There was something disarming—almost magical—about the way she opened her world to him without hesitation, as if trusting him with pieces of her soul no one else had ever been allowed to touch. No girl had ever spoken to him with such effortless sincerity.

Whenever Swetha talked, her facial expressions—the way her eyelashes fluttered and then relaxed, and how she often tucked her hair behind her ears mesmerized him. Eventually, they reached Lonavala. Madhavi was walking next to Swetha though Rahul wanted to be in that place. Lonavala was lush with greenery, misty meadows all around. It was a soothing sight for the eyes. From June to September, it rains almost 24/7 there. That day was no exception, a slight drizzle and a pleasant chill in the air.

What they had come for was an engagement function. Whether there would be time to visit nearby tourist attractions like Kune Falls, Karla Caves, and Bhaja Caves was uncertain. Rahul softly suggested to Swetha,

"Shall we also check out some nearby places?" Swetha smiled and said, "You go, visit, and come back." For Rahul, the sightseeing wasn't important. What mattered was seeing those places *with* Swetha.

Just then, a call came from Apoorva. Apoorva had booked rooms for everyone at a resort named Della. The engagement function was scheduled to be held at another renowned resort, Radisson.

There was approximately a four-kilometer distance between the place of stay and the function venue. Madhavi was explaining this to Swetha. They entered the Della Resort. At the reception, a staff member greeted them: "Good morning. Welcome to Della Resort." A total of 34 rooms had been booked the receptionist said.

The rent for a single room is ₹26,000. (Rahul did notice the leaflet on the desk) Rahul quickly did a mental calculation—at this rate, they must have spent at least ₹8,00,000 just for this engagement function. And then the thought struck him:

What am I going to do for my wedding?

At the reception desk, Swetha, Madhavi, and Rahul were waiting. No names were being called out. Each room was allotted for two people. Anyone could collect the key in their name and share the room. The receptionist called their names Swetha stepped forward, collected the key—*Room No. 529.* The corridor buzzed softly with laughter and footsteps. Who would be sharing the room with her? Madhavi and Rahul stood close by, waiting for the moment to decide. Swetha turned to Rahul, her eyes calm, her voice almost a whisper.

"Are you coming?"

For a heartbeat, Rahul hesitated. And in that heartbeat, Madhavi pulled her American Tourister trolley forward. "I'll come," Madhavi said quickly, stepping ahead. The two women disappeared down the hallway, their laughter fading like a retreating tune. Something inside Rahul sank.

Should I have just said yes? Quickly... That familiar hesitation— always thinking twice, always holding back— he sighed. The culture that he comes from..

Maybe it's his experience from Chennai.

He walked to his own room, the key cold in his hand. The city outside glowed through the curtains, sleepless and distant. But inside, the night refused to rest. The mattress promised comfort—*Sleep Factory Mattress*— He switched on the TV, Actor Anil Kapoor is talking about the good sleep that you will have in the Smart Grid Technology mattress. The same mattress was in his cot. yet he kept turning, lost in thought. He switched off the TV and tried to sleep.

Every time he closed his eyes, he saw Swetha. Her voice, her smile, her question— looping endlessly in his mind. The next day was the main function The hotel reception hall buzzed with laughter and bright conversations as everyone gathered, ready for the main function. A minibus waited outside, but Rahul barely noticed it. His friends spoke around him, joked around him, but his mind was elsewhere. His eyes kept drifting, searching for one face.

Then, from the far end of the hall, the elevator chimed. The doors parted, and Swetha stepped out. For Rahul it was like a movie.

She walked forward with the kind of effortless grace that didn't announce itself, yet commanded attention all the same. She tossed her hair back casually, unaware that the tiny gesture could undo a man so completely. She looked like a Ravi Varma painting brought into the present—radiant, modern, yet touched with a classical beauty that felt timeless.

Her navy blue lehenga shimmered softly with every step she took, the elegant cut of her blouse revealing a delicate line of her back that made Rahul's breath catch. Her straightened hair fell like a sleek, glossy curtain, framing her face in a way that could make any passerby believe she belonged on a magazine cover.

And Swetha walked straight to Rahul.

"How am I looking today?" He was speechless.

"You look… different," he said.

"Different? Not nice?" she asked, frowning.

"No,no! You look absolutely beautiful," he stammered.

Was this the same Swetha he saw every day?

She had always been pretty, but today… with all the makeup and styling, she looked like a heroine straight out of a Hindi film. Madhavi came near… Madhavi exclaimed,

"Wow! Is this a designer piece?" Swetha replied,

"No, no—this one is just for Apoorva's engagement. For my wedding,

I've shortlisted a Tarun Tahiliani embroidered piece." Or "Papa Don't Preach" Lehengas …. Madhavi gasped.

"That alone would cost at least five lakhs!"

What is this madness?

When it comes to weddings, women will turn men's lives upside down,

Rahul thought to himself.

Rahul looked at Swetha and said,

"You look like. Deepika Padukone "

"Oh, thanks!" she simply laughed but, in her heart she was very happy.

Then, moving closer, she said, "Come, let's go." They sat next to each other on the minibus. When Rahul stuck his head out to feel the breeze, his hair got a little messy. Swetha noticed and gently ran her fingers through it, tidying it.

To Rahul, this was an entirely new experience. No girl had ever come that close to him. No one had ever touched his hair.

But could this alone be taken as love?

One step near to girl friend ?

Girls these days—especially those who grow up in Pune and Mumbai—don't differentiate between boys and girls the way people used to.

Everyone is a "friend." for them.

There's a fine line between being friendly and being in love. But understanding and interpreting that line is incredibly difficult.

On stage, beneath a canopy of soft lights and shimmering decorations, Arpan and Apoorva looked almost ethereal—glowing with the quiet radiance that newlyweds often carried, as though touched by something celestial. Arpan's favorite sister Ria was also standing on the stage and receiving guests one by one and facilitating them to reach the couple.

Woman around 75 years of age Jaya aunty walked towards Ria and asked,

" Next is your turn ?"

Ria said Aunty .. I wanted to achieve many things in Medicine. I don't have time to think about marriage now.

Let us enjoy today and leave happily.

The main difference between the previous generation and the current generation is the aged uncles and aunties will ask any personal questions to the youngsters without any hesitation.

When are you getting married?

How much is your salary?

If married, then they will ask

what are your plans for children?

It's normal to see some Jaya aunties in any marriage.

The way Ria spoke that Jaya aunty slowly moved on the other side and found another young girl and started asking the similar questions.

On the stage,

Guests formed a proper line, moving up one after another to embrace the couple, offer gifts wrapped with affection, and smile for the waiting camera. Laughter floated through the air like champagne bubbles. In the midst of it all, Rahul and Swetha drew their own share of attention.

Every person who approached them glanced at Swetha and paused for a heartbeat, admiration lighting up their faces.

"You look gorgeous… like a princess," they told her, again and again. Swetha responded with her trademark smile—graceful, poised.

But Rahul saw something deeper behind it: that tender spark of joy women feel when they are truly seen, appreciated.

It glimmered in her eyes, soft and unmistakably genuine, as though each compliment settled warmly in her heart. Soon it was their turn to walk onto the stage. They congratulated the newlyweds, exchanged a few words, and moved for the photograph. The photographer looked through his lens, frowned lightly, and motioned with a practiced hand.

"You're not in the frame—please come closer," he instructed.

Then, with a laugh, he added in Hindi, "Aur thoda… closer!" Rahul and Swetha exchanged a tiny, helpless glance—and obeyed.

They shifted closer, the space between them narrowing until they gently bumped against one another. Swetha's shoulder brushed his, light as a whisper but powerful enough to send a shiver through him.

Her perfume—subtle, feminine, a little intoxicating—wrapped around him like an invisible ribbon. Her shoulder grazed his again, almost touching, almost lingering.

And suddenly, something unfamiliar fluttered inside him. What was this strange feeling ?
A feeling that he had never known before. After the photo session, they walked down to the dining hall.

The place was buzzing with laughter, chatter, and the clatter of plates. Everything was beautifully arranged, yet crowded—tables filling up faster than they could spot one. After nearly ten minutes of waiting, Rahul and Swetha finally managed to find seats beside each other. They had shared dinners before—after movies, on casual evenings out—but tonight it felt different. There was a quiet magic in the air, something unspoken between them.

The waiters drifted through the hall like a well-rehearsed ballet, their trays filled with small bowls of warm, fragrant Gulab Jamun—the one sweet no Indian wedding was complete without.
One of them paused briefly at Rahul and Swetha's table, placing a bowl before Rahul before sweeping away again, never noticing he had missed her.

Rahul had just taken his first bite when Swetha looked at him, her voice soft but unmistakably wistful.

"That's my favorite."
He immediately shifted, ready to call after the waiter, but before the words even formed, she leaned forward with effortless boldness—so natural it felt as if she had always belonged in his space.
With a playful glint in her eyes, she plucked the half-eaten Gulab Jamun straight from his bowl and popped it into her mouth, smiling with unguarded delight. For an instant, Rahul went completely still.

A stolen bite, a shared sweetness, a small intimacy that felt far larger than the moment deserved.

And then it happened: a warmth spread through him, gentle at first, then deeper, richer. It flowed not just through his chest but through every corner of him, light as laughter and sweet as honey.

It had nothing to do with dessert, nothing to do with sugar. It felt like something had shifted—quietly, irrevocably. A sweetness that wasn't on his tongue but in his veins. A warmth that wasn't from the Gulab Jamun but from her—the girl sitting beside him, grinning, unaware of the havoc she had just created in his heart.

After dinner, they stepped out, only to realize that the resort's mini-bus had already left. The next one wouldn't arrive for another hour. Swetha looked at him and smiled. "Let's just take an Uber instead of waiting." Rahul nodded, and soon they were on their way. The car moved slowly along the winding hill-station road. Outside, the mist hung low; streetlights shimmered faintly through the fog. Inside, silence settled between them—a quiet comfort filled with unspoken words. The road was rough and uneven, still under repair. Every bump, every turn made them shift a little closer. Their shoulders brushed now and then, lightly, unintentionally—yet neither moved away. At one sharp curve, the driver accelerated, and Swetha instinctively reached out, steadying herself. Another sharp turn, the driver accelerated too quickly. Swetha instinctively reached for Rahul's hand to steady herself.

She came very close to him—face to face—and suddenly pressed her lips against his lips.

"Today, I'm very happy," she whispered.

For Rahul, this was the *first kiss.*

A pleasure he had never experienced before. It was as if an electric current surged through his body. Her hand lingered near his for a moment longer than necessary.

When she looked up, their eyes met—steady, searching, uncertain. The rest of the ride passed in silence. When they finally reached the resort, they stepped out and walked back to their rooms, the night air cool, and their hearts strangely full.

After that, neither of them said a word. Eventually, they returned to their rooms. But Rahul couldn't sleep. His mind was unsettled.

Looking back at everything that had happened that day …

-the stories she shared about her childhood during the train ride… …

-her entrance in the stunning lehenga and asking, "How do I look?" …

-the bite from the Gulab Jamun she playfully ate from his plate… …

-the way they stood shoulder-to-shoulder for the photo and finally,

-the kiss on his lips —

when he tried putting all the pieces together like Jigsaw puzzle one question repeatedly came to his mind

What did all this mean?

Was it love?

With today's women, one must read carefully.

She might turn around and say,

"I didn't feel anything. It was all just for fun." Even when they returned to Mumbai the next day, Swetha spoke as if *nothing* had happened. But for

Rahul, the previous day replayed over and over in his head.

For her, everything was normal. Back to classes, back to project discussions. For Rahul, it was different … He even began scoring less marks in the weekly internal tests, every Wednesday.

Meanwhile, Swetha—as always—scored high. How could she manage to focus as though nothing had happened?

That's the difference between men and women,
Rahul realized.
Even a small emotional event could send a man spiraling into endless thoughts and fantasies, losing touch with reality.
But for women?

They could experience something significant and carry on as though nothing had happened.
The saying "Don't share secrets with women" is a lie.
Women can keep secrets. They can lock their feelings deep inside and continue life as usual. But a man can't.
Time moved quietly, and before they knew it, the final year had begun.
After being together for three years, one afternoon, out of nowhere,
Swetha asked Rahul, "Hey… why don't we take this forward? Why don't we get married?"
For a moment, Rahul froze.
He had imagined this conversation countless times—the setting, the words, the feeling of hearing her say

it. But now that it had actually happened, and she was the one to say it first, a strange sense of defeat settled over him.

She beat me to it. This time too ....

Seeing his startled expression, Swetha smiled lightly. "No rush," she said. "Take a couple of days to think about it." Her calmness left him more unsettled than her question.

How could she be so casual about something so big? he thought.

That night, sleep refused to come. He lay awake, thoughts spinning in circles— his parents' faces flashing in his mind.

We sent you to Mumbai to study—and now this? What would Mom think?

His father, he knew, wouldn't be too difficult. If his mother agreed, his father would quietly follow. Most of the south Indian couples whom he has seen are like this. Men look strong on the outside, but the final decision is always taken by the woman.

Convincing his mother... that would be the real test.

The next morning, with a heart full of hope and a touch of nervous courage, Rahul finally brought up Swetha's name while speaking to his mother.

He had prepared himself for a storm of questions, perhaps even a long silence heavy with disapproval. But instead, her answer was calm, almost unexpectedly kind. "She's a Tamil girl, isn't she? Then everything will be fine," his mother said, her voice gentle. "Don't burden your heart with worry." For a moment, Rahul simply closed his eyes, letting the relief sweep through him. It felt as if a door he had feared for so long had quietly opened.

Later, when he met Swetha, the joy inside him was impossible to hide. "I'm ready for the wedding," he told her, the words spilling out of him with a certainty he had never felt before. "I want to continue this relationship.

Let's get married." Swetha looked at him with that soft, knowing smile—one that always seemed to calm the storms within him. "It's okay at your house," she said playfully.

"But what about mine?" Then, in a tone filled with quiet assurance, she added,

"If I speak to my parents, they won't say no. My happiness means everything to them." Her confidence steadied him even more than his mother's blessing. Yet she wasn't in a hurry, and that grounded grace was one of the many things he loved about her.
"Let's finish our studies," she said softly.

"Let's find good jobs, build something strong, and then think about marriage." Rahul nodded, understanding not just her words but the wisdom behind them. And in that moment, it felt as though their future—bright, patient, and beautifully certain—had already begun.

As the final year was approaching, campus interviews were happening on one side, and many students were applying to American universities for higher studies. Swetha downloaded the University application forms and applied to several programs and insisted that Rahul do the same. Rahul hesitated. She was talking about Ivy League. The Ivy League is an athletic conference of eight private universities in the Northeastern United States, known for their academic excellence, prestige, and selective admissions. The eight member schools are Brown University, Columbia University, Cornell University, Dartmouth College, Harvard University, Princeton University, the University of Pennsylvania, and Yale University. The term "Ivy League" originally referred to the "ivy-covered campuses" ..

She started explaining but nothing registered to Rahul He was simply looking at her style of talking. At the same time, in the back of his mind, his thought went back to his parents.

His parents believed that once he got a job, their family's financial struggles would ease. How could I tell them I want to study abroad?

Surprisingly, this time, his father was completely supportive. "If you study in America, you'll earn well. Our family's situation will improve. You can get your sisters married in a lavish manner. Your mother and I can even come visit you like your uncle does with his son," his father said. But his mother had a different concern. "Go wherever you want," she said. "Just get married before you leave."

Now, how would he explain this to Swetha?

He was polarized inside. The next day, when he met her, he said,

"What if we get married first and then go to the U.S. together?" Swetha replied,

"Do you think going to America for studies is that simple?" "If we get the opportunity, we must go immediately. We can get married any time," said Swetha. Rahul thought, "We're both thinking about this so much... wouldn't her parents be thinking about it too?"

In most families, when women are given freedom, the entire household transforms. Happiness naturally grows.

Girls who treat their fathers and brothers with respectful ease rather than fearful obedience usually turn out to be incredibly capable.

Any family where women live without fear and with joy will certainly thrive.

Swetha was a woman from one such family. Rahul's family is not as progressive as Swetha's. In life, what we go chasing after is often running toward us as well.

If we approach everything positively, life tends to unfold positively. Despite all the forms Rahul filled out and the hopes he carried, nothing turned out as he had imagined when it came to getting into an American university. Meanwhile, Swetha got accepted to both University of Cincinnati and Boston University. She was thrilled and began preparing to leave. Rahul applied for jobs in Chennai, Ahmedabad, and Bengaluru.

Being an IIT graduate, he got offers from all three. While his parents wanted him to choose Chennai, Swetha insisted the Ahmedabad job was the better option. She also added, "Anyway, I won't be able to live in Chennai.

We will be living in two different cities. Rahul didn't know what to say—his response was simply silence. Swetha sat next to her parents.

Her parents had a calm conversation with her about going to U.S. Her mother gently said, "It's fine that you're going abroad, but at least get married here at home before you go." Her father added,

"Why don't you just get married and then go?" Swetha thought her parents were so modern and now she felt that they are typical Indian parents.

They both knew one thing clearly—once Swetha made up her mind, it was nearly impossible to change it. Still, they thought it was worth expressing their wishes. But they also knew, whatever she decides, it will always be the right decision.

In life, what we assume to be easy often turns out to be difficult. What we assume to be difficult sometimes unfolds with ease. And that's exactly what happened here in Swetha's house. No one knew what went through Swetha's mind, but she simply said, "Okay, Dad,

I'll get married and then go to the U.S."

When it comes to women raised with complete freedom, you can never predict what decision they might take. But when it's time to make one, they'll always make the right call.

Swetha's decision was one of those.

She had to leave for Cincinnati by August 18th. So, they fixed the wedding for June. Every decision was Swetha's. And yet, Rahul felt happy.

As the wedding day neared, Swetha calculated the wedding budget to be around ₹30 lakhs. Rahul couldn't even fathom that amount. He hesitantly said to her,

"Why don't we keep our wedding simple?"

The parents were discussing to have the marriage in Anna Nagar Chennai. Swetha replied, since childhood, I've always dreamt of a "***destination wedding***".

And now we're getting married in this tiny little Anna Nagar." To her, Anna Nagar seemed too small. Rahul thought, Why Anna Nagar at all? If we find a wedding hall somewhere in a suburb, the expenses could be even lower.

But for Swetha, all expenses must be split 50-50 between the bride and groom.

That's how modern women think. Whether it's household expenses or changing a baby's diaper, everything must be equal. "We earn too, don't we? Then why should we do all the work alone?" they say. Swetha even told Rahul,

"You should go to the beauty parlor too." for the wedding. For her, weddings weren't just about women spending thousands to get their skin and hair treated, men should do it too. Just the beauty salon budget could exceed ₹1 lakh. In today's weddings, there's also a *pre-wedding shoot.* The bride and groom go to a resort, pose for romantic pictures and videos. Those alone cost nearly ₹3 lakhs.

Rahul went along with it.

They went to a posh bridal saree store Moksha in Alwarpet, Chennai, just to choose Swetha's reception saree.

It seemed like a place reserved only for the ultra-rich.

But as they entered, Rahul saw many middle-class people browsing designer pieces. Inside, a young staff member greeted them and asked,

"What budget are you looking at?" Swetha responded confidently, "There's no budget as such. I'll just tell you, my expectations."

"I'm looking for a blouse with intricate hand embroidery, glittering stones, and traditional motifs. A *timeless saree* with vibrant colours made of rich silk fabrics."

Rahul understood barely half of what she said.

As far as he was concerned, a costly silk saree meant going to T. Nagar—Pothys or RMKV usual popularly known Textile shops for middle class people. Anything over ₹30,000 would make him nervous.

This is a rule written only for the middle class. You have to walk into stores meant for the rich — people who shop without even knowing where the money comes from. It is an expensive affair, Yet, you must count every single rupee before you spend it. Even before getting married and taking up the responsibilities of a family man,

Why, were there already so much expense? Perhaps this is why many men hesitate when it comes to marriage. While Rahul was lost in thought, Swetha came up to him with a bright smile. "Everything's available here! I wasn't sure if we'd find in Chennai what we usually get in Mumbai or Pune. But this place is superb," she said.

For Swetha, the shopping trip had been nothing short of exhilarating. She moved through the aisles with the confidence of a woman who knew exactly what she wanted, and by the time they reached the counter, the bill touched three lakh rupees. Rahul tried to smile, convincing himself that this would be the biggest expense of the wedding.

A stretch — yes — but manageable. But he was wrong. Very wrong. Just as he let out a quiet sigh of relief, Swetha turned to him and said brightly,

"Next, we'll go to the GRT jewelry store in T. Nagar." He blinked. "For what?

The thali chain (they call it Mangalsutra in North India) is already bought. My parents got it last month." "I know," she said, her tone light, almost casual.

"I want a diamond pendant to go with it."

A diamond pendant?

Rahul felt the ground shift beneath him. He had walked into the store GRT thinking he might spend another hundred thousand at most — one last splurge before the wedding.

But as the sales girl unveiled tray after tray, Swetha's eyes settled on a single, elegant piece. Gold–Diamond Pendant EF VVS 861.

The pendant gleamed under the showroom lights, a delicate 22kt yellow gold design weighing 5.880 grams, with seventeen tiny diamonds flawlessly arranged around it.

The salesgirl's voice flowed like a soft melody as she explained: round shape cut, colour EF, clarity VVS, carat weight 1.410.

Rahul barely heard the details.

He only saw the price. Three hundred and thirty-nine thousand rupees. Nearly another three and a half

lakhs. As Swetha admired the piece with a quiet sigh of delight, Rahul felt his bank accounts thinning in his mind, one after another, like candles flickering out. Three days left for the wedding… And he was already stretched to the breaking point. Yet, watching her eyes glow with happiness, watching the way she touched the pendant as though imagining her future in it, he didn't say a word.

Love had its own strange arithmetic — one that didn't always add up.

Finally, the wedding day arrived. The hall was bright, filled with colour, music, the murmur of families blending into one another. Rahul stood at the stage with a heart full of emotions he could barely name — relief, exhaustion, hope, love. And when he looked at Swetha, radiant in her bridal silk, he saw the same joy reflected in her eyes. The ceremonies went smoothly, every ritual unfolding with a grace that felt almost fated.

In the end, all the expenses, all the running around, all the sleepless nights faded into the background. Because in that moment, as the sacred knot was tied and the hall erupted into blessing and applause, Rahul felt only one thing — that everything had finally come together.

On the wedding day, Swetha's divine look made Rahul's relatives and Chennai friends whisper into his ears,
"She looks just like Film actress Trisha in a Pothys silk saree TV advertisement — absolutely stunning!" Rahul leaned closer, his breath warm against Swetha's ear, his voice barely more than a whisper.

"You look so beautiful in this saree," he murmured, unable to hide the awe in his eyes.

"The saree, the blouse… they bring out your grace in a way nothing else does. You should wear sarees more often."

Swetha laughed softly, the sound light and unbothered. "That's enough with sarees for today," she said, shaking her head. "Don't expect me to make a habit of it. I'm happiest in jeans and a T-shirt, and you know it."

In the name of freedom, many modern women hesitate to embrace even simple gestures—gestures that have the power to strengthen and reaffirm the very foundation of a marital bond.

The wedding expenses had crossed twenty-five lakh rupees. Wherever Rahul couldn't afford to spend, Swetha did it herself.

Rahul began to feel that familiar sense of inferiority again. Had they wanted too much? This is the story of almost every man today. The moment marriage arrives, they extend their hands to bear the weight of it. They borrow money and spend lavishly, thinking, *It's a once-in-a-lifetime event.* Rahul, too, had been pushed into the same situation. "Let's just be happy today. Tomorrow's struggles can wait till tomorrow," he thought.

It was their first night after the wedding. Rahul waited, filled with dreams and anticipation. Swetha walked in and said,

"Dear… I'm very tired. Let's sleep." Rahul suggested softly, "Let's just talk for a while." "We'll have plenty of time to talk on our honeymoon the day after tomorrow," she replied.

In the midst of all the excitement and the endless rituals that followed their wedding, Swetha faced another responsibility — one that held the promise of an entirely different future. She had to submit her passport at the American Consulate in Chennai.

The night before, she sat on the edge of the bed, meticulously arranging every document she might need: the crisp university offer letter, the carefully printed bank statements showing proof of funds, and the many small but essential papers she had gathered over the past few months. Each sheet represented a dream, a possibility, a doorway into the life she was preparing to build.

The next morning, as the sun crept over Anna Salai, she stood outside the towering walls of the U.S. Consulate. A sea of students had already gathered, forming a line that seemed to stretch endlessly down the pavement. They had been standing there since daybreak — young men and women clutching hopes far bigger than the folders in their hands.

India was often called a poor country, and yet, as Swetha looked at those determined faces and the hundred-strong queue brimming with ambition, she couldn't help but think how untrue that sounded.

A nation that sent so many of its children across oceans in pursuit of knowledge didn't look poor at all — it looked courageous.

She had joined the line at 5:00 a.m., and by the time she stepped inside the consulate a little after eight, her nerves had been replaced by a quiet calm. Her documents were flawless; she had prepared for this moment with the same discipline she brought to every part of her life.

At the counter, the American officer gave her a brief glance, then another, flipping through her papers with practiced efficiency. And then he looked up, his expression softening into a reassuring smile. "All the best. You may go. We'll get back to you."

It was just a simple sentence, almost routine for him — but for her, it was everything. Those few words carried the unmistakable weight of approval.

And as she stepped out into the bright Chennai morning, Swetha felt something lift inside her — a lightness, a certainty, as if the future had just quietly opened its doors. Swetha was overjoyed. She came straight to Rahul who was waiting outside, coiled her arms around Rahul's neck, and shared the happy news. Rahul was thrilled too, though a small sadness lingered — the thought that he would have to live apart from her for a few months.

At last, her long-held dream of studying in America was coming true.

They had planned a honeymoon in Bali or Switzerland, but with all the visa formalities and preparations taking up so much time, they finally settled for Ooty which is nearby.

Sterling Holiday Resorts – Ooty Tamilnadu.

The resort buzzed with upper-middle-class families — parents with two children running about, middle-aged couples who had brought their elderly parents for a break, and three or four young newlywed couples like Rahul and Swetha. The reception area was crowded and lively. After completing the check-in formalities, Rahul and Swetha stepped into Room No. 108 — their little haven in the quiet hills of Ooty.

"Finally," Swetha sighed, sinking into the soft mattress with the exhaustion of travel and the lingering shimmer of newlywed excitement.

Rahul sat beside her, brushing a gentle hand over hers. "Shall we bathe and then eat?

Or eat first and go boating on the lake?" he asked softly, as though afraid to disturb the delicate sweetness of the moment.

He had held her hand a thousand times during their college days, but now, it felt transformed — warmer, more precious, carrying the weight of something irrevocably theirs.

When he lay down beside her, she instinctively rested her arm on his shoulder. The crisp cold of Ooty drifted in through the windows, making the warmth between them feel even more intimate, more magnetic. Their closeness deepened in quiet, unspoken ways — the kind of closeness that couldn't be measured in distance, only in heartbeat. The tenderness they shared melted the space between them, filling the room with a sweetness he had never known before.

In college, the simple brush of her fingers against his had been enough to thrill him for days. But now, feeling her lean into him, feeling her breath mingle with his — it felt like stepping into a dream he had carried for years.

At one point, Swetha reached for the thali (the sacred gold chain mangalsuthra) around her neck, unfastened it, and placed it gently on the side table. "It's pricking me," she murmured. Rahul blinked, surprised. All his life, he had seen women treat the thali chain with a reverence bordering on sacred. His mother touched it to her eyes every morning after circling the Tulsi plant (sacred Plant Hindus do pooja on a daily basis after bath)— never once removing it lightly.

Who was this woman he had married? he wondered.

Was she the "modern woman" like famous Tamil Poet Bharathi had once written about — bold, self-aware, quietly independent?

Or was she the traditional woman his mother and grandmother had been — devoted, gentle, rooted in rituals? No… Swetha stood somewhere in between.

A blend of freedom and familiarity, of modern thoughts wrapped in timeless grace. Their college memories floated back — the laughter, the longing, even the tiny misunderstandings that had once felt so important. Now, they dissolved effortlessly, as if love had washed the slate clean.

There was a sweetness in the thought:

" You for me, and I for you "

Wrapped in the privacy of their honeymoon room, unaware of the world outside, they rediscovered one another — not as classmates, not as two young people navigating a fragile love, but as partners finally stepping into the life they had chosen together.

Life felt astonishingly generous in that moment. Afterward, they freshened up and walked to the lake for boating. The sky was turning a dusky blue; dinner was still hours away. They returned to their room with the quiet glow of two people discovering a new rhythm together — and once again, they found themselves drawn to each other, as naturally as breathing.

Later, after dinner, they watched television for a while, their shoulders touching, the comfort between them easy and warm. When they finally turned in for the night, Swetha felt a flutter of hesitation — a whisper of "Not again…" mingled with another voice, softer, surer, saying "Yes."

Rahul reached for her gently. The night deepened around them, tender and full of promise — the beginning of a journey neither of them would ever forget.

"For our first child, would you prefer a boy or a girl?" Rahul asked gently.

Without a moment's hesitation, Swetha replied,
"I like all children. But I don't want us to have any. Raising a child, taking care of it every day — it's such a struggle.
For the next ten years, we won't be able to focus on our careers. And after that, there's no need to have children at all. So… I don't want any."
Rahul was stunned. He hadn't expected that. How could a woman say she didn't want children?
All the women he had known while growing up had placed great value on motherhood. But modern women — they seemed to see motherhood as a burden.

He wanted to tell her,
That's impossible. We must have a child.

But before he could speak, Swetha said firmly, "There's no need to discuss it now. If anyone has the right to decide, it's me. I'm the one who has to carry the baby, after all. So, the decision is mine." Anger rose within Rahul. But just then, Swetha came close, wrapped her arms around him, and pressed a kiss on his lips.

The moment she kissed him, Rahul felt an overwhelming surge of pleasure — one he wasn't ready to let go of.

This is where men fall, he thought. And women — they know it all too well.

Was married life truly this blissful? And yet, at the same time, it felt... complicated.

Though there were moments of emotional joy and confusion, physically, those four days were filled with happiness.

Then they returned to Chennai. In just a week, all the arrangements for Swetha's U.S. departure had to be completed. Swetha began preparing for her journey to America.

From Chennai, she had already come down to Pune. As usual, she had spread out all her clothes on the bed and sat in the middle, trying to decide which ones to iron and which to pack as they were.

Just then, the little girl from the opposite apartment — Ria— came running in. From the time she was born, Ria had adored Swetha. And Swetha loved the child deeply, too. Whenever they were together, she would lose track of time, completely absorbed in play. Even when Ria's mother, Kinjal, came calling for her, the little girl would close her eyes and cling tightly to Swetha's neck, refusing to let go. Such was their affection for each other. Swetha would give Ria anything she reached out for. From morning till evening, the little girl would be at Swetha's place. Now and then, her mother, Kinjal, would come over, coax and cajole her, and finally take her back home. If a single day passed without seeing Swetha, Ria would throw a tantrum — she wouldn't eat, wouldn't sleep. It had become a part of their daily routine.

Now, the thought of going away to America for two years weighed heavily on Swetha's heart.

But even more than her, it troubled Kinjal — she worried constantly about how her child would manage without Swetha.

Only in India, neighbor's living next door grow so close that they become like one family. It's common here to treat the neighbor's child as one's own — to pamper, scold, and shower them with affection. Putting aside all her packing, Swetha began playing with Ria once again. Her heart felt a little lighter.

No matter how exciting the thought of higher studies was, the idea of living away from Rahul — and from her parents — for two whole years brought a quiet ache in Swetha's heart.

That ache had now been eased a little. By August 1st, Rahul had already joined his new job in Ahmedabad.

On the 18th, at 8:00 p.m., Swetha's Emirates flight was scheduled to depart from Mumbai International airport. From Pune, she planned to travel the previous evening, stay overnight at her friend's house in Bandra, and leave for the airport by 4:00 p.m. the next day.

Rahul had promised, "I'll come from Ahmedabad by morning or at least by noon." But it was a new job, and despite his best efforts, he couldn't leave at the time he had hoped. He caught a train from Ahmedabad to Mumbai, and by the time he reached, it was already 5:00 p.m.

From the Mumbai railway station, he booked an Uber cab to Chhatrapati Shivaji Airport. Being a Saturday evening, the traffic was unbearable — vehicles crawled forward like ants. Rahul knew he wouldn't make it on time.

He called Swetha on the phone. She, having waited for him so long, was fuming with anger. "All the check-in formalities are done," she said sharply. "Only the

immigration check is left. There's still a little time." If she delayed any longer, she would miss the flight.

Brushing away the tears that welled up in her eyes, Swetha moved toward the immigration office. Once on the plane, she would have to switch off her phone. That meant they wouldn't be able to speak for the next 18 hours.

Even small misunderstandings between a husband and wife can be resolved quickly if addressed immediately. A few hours of silence might be tolerable, but if it stretches longer, anger builds — and later, mending it requires much effort.

When Rahul learned the flight had departed, he left the airport, his mind heavy with confusion. Swetha's parents, walking nearby, didn't say a word. Part of them worried that their daughter was travelling alone, yet they understood she was determined. No matter how many reasons Rahul gave for not arriving on time, they were calm.

In life, it isn't the effort we make that counts the most, but the final destination we arrive at matters.

Rahul returned to Ahmedabad, burdened with both frustration and regret. The senior manager at his new company, Harish Mehta said "Hi".

Rahul was furious at him for not being able to leave on time due to the company's newly assigned work. He did not reply and simply went to his seat.

After an 18-hour journey, Swetha finally landed at the Cincinnati Airport. From there, she took an Uber to the university. A new place, unfamiliar faces, and an unimaginable chill in the air. Though thought of Rahul crossed her mind, she hardly had the time to dwell on anything else. The next day was Sunday.

Her first day of college would be on Monday. On a quiet Sunday afternoon, Swetha found herself preparing for yet another new experience. Her cousin Sundar — a relative she had spoken to many times but never met in person — had invited her over for lunch. The idea of meeting family she barely knew made her both curious and strangely uneasy.

Exactly at one o'clock, Sundar arrived at her hostel, cheerful and punctual, and drove her to his home. Everything about this new world felt unfamiliar to her — new relationships, new manners of speaking, even new expectations. All the Tamil relatives, she noticed with mild surprise, conversed entirely in English, as though clinging to a bridge between two cultures. Sundar's wife, Nirali, welcomed her warmly. Their little boy, Vivaan, peeked at her shyly from behind a doorway. And then came the largest surprise of all — a puppy so enormous it seemed more calf than a dog. The creature trotted up to Swetha, tail wagging wildly, as though greeting an old friend.

Sundar laughed. "First rule — don't call her 'dog.' She has a name. Ziwi."

He added with a mischievous smile, "Even back home, they say if there's enough love, even a dog can become human… and sometimes a human can become a dog." Swetha couldn't help smiling.

The warmth of the room brought back memories of Pune — her friend affectionately calling her own pet Jamila or Kuttimma, and the same girl, during fights with her brother, yelling, "Poda patti!" "Patti " means in their mother-tongue Malayalam language is Dog The contradictions of affection and irritation suddenly felt universal.

But here in America, Swetha discovered, life moved by different rules. Dogs weren't merely pets; they were woven into the very fabric of a family's heart. Sundar explained gently how couples arranged their schedules around them — weekend trips, grocery runs, even simple dinners out. And if ever they left the dog behind, a quiet anxiety followed them everywhere.

Did she eat? Did she sleep? Is she lonely?

As though sensing the conversation was about her, little Zivi nudged her warm nose into Swetha's palm. Swetha brushed her fingers over the silky fur, surprised by the tenderness that rose inside her — soft, unexpected, almost childlike. "This one," Sundar

said with unmistakable pride, "rings a bell when she needs to go out. Never touches a thing unless we tell her she can. She's as smart as a child. And we set aside a separate monthly budget just for her.
More than a thousand dollars."

Just then, a light tapping sounded at the door — the eager paw of Casper, the neighbor's dog. Moments later, Devika, the neighbor and Nirali's friend, laughed as she stepped inside. "Our Casper can't stay away from Zivi," she said fondly. "They're best friends." Swetha watched the two animals, their joy simple and pure, and her eyes widened with a quiet question.
"What happens when she grows old?" she asked softly, her voice tinged with the realism she carried from home.

"In India... when you grow older even the final days for people themselves are so difficult."
A shadow of sorrow slipped across Sundar's face. "Maybe in India," he said gently. "But here... when life becomes too painful, when the bills, the suffering, the weight of it all becomes too much, everyone gathers. Family, friends. They take the pet to the vet. People leave work... they all come. The vet gives a final injection." His voice softened into a whisper. "And they say goodbye. Peacefully. Gently. With love."

Swetha fell silent. Her thoughts wandered — across continents, across cultures, across the fragile line between love and loss. Whether in India or in the U.S., she realized, the truth remained the same:

humans love their pets with a thread of selfishness — wanting comfort, loyalty, companionship.

But a pet… a pet loves without asking for anything at all. Unconditional Love. May be true… Swetha nodded, listening, but her thoughts had already drifted miles away — back to Rahul.

The moment she stepped out of Sundar's home and returned to her hostel room, a single thought filled her heart: I should call him…

I must apologize. Surely he was upset that he had reached the airport late. But when she checked the time, it was already 5:00 p.m. in Cincinnati — past midnight in Ahmedabad India. Calling now might disturb him, she reasoned. I'll call him tomorrow morning, she decided, placing her phone aside. And in that quiet decision, her heart carried both longing and regret — emotions that followed her gently into the night. The next morning was her first day of classes. Finding her way around the vast university campus—locating the right hall, the lecture schedule, the professor—took up all her time. She couldn't call Rahul but was pining.

At least I can send a message, she thought, and typed on WhatsApp:

"Reached safely. How are you?"

The next three days went by in a blur of lectures and campus routines. Between Swetha and Rahul, the WhatsApp messages carried a quiet bitterness—sharp words wrapped in polite sentences, each one landing slightly off-mark. Messages travelled back and forth, blue ticks appearing instantly, but neither of them made the one gesture that mattered: calling. Some conversations, life insisted, were never meant to happen through typed words.

No matter how heartfelt the message, how carefully chosen the sentence, no one could ever predict how the person on the other side might read it. Tone vanished. Warmth vanished. Only assumptions remained.

And so, it was with them. Every line Rahul typed—sometimes frustrated, sometimes pleading—Swetha read with her own interpretation, shaped by distance, exhaustion, and old hurt. Her replies, too, came edged with meanings she never intended. And the argument, which should have quietly ended, began spiraling into something bigger, older, heavier.

Their misunderstanding drifted back—not to this week, not to this moment—but to that night in Ooty, when they had spoken about children. *He had said he wanted one. She had insisted the decision rested with her.* Now, those old words resurfaced like ghosts, dragged into a conversation that had nothing to do with them. Unnecessary sentences piled up on both sides, gathering weight, gathering heat.

Who should speak first?

Who should listen? Was it you? Was it me? Equality—so beautifully phrased in books, so reassuring in theory—felt painfully fragile in real life, where emotions were uneven, and people were imperfect. Rahul, already battling a quiet sense of inadequacy he never admitted aloud, let that vulnerability slip into his tone. His replies grew sharper, colder—unintentionally cruel. It was as though he were pouring oil on a flame he desperately wished would go out.

And somewhere between the lines, the two of them drifted further apart—not out of lack of love, but out of the sheer inability to say what they truly meant. He began to wonder if all these questions should have been asked before marriage. Back then, they had only talked about studies, academics, and careers—never once about whether they truly wanted marriage or children afterwards. Neither of them had thought to ask.

That night, it was Friday for Rahul. He felt he had to talk to her—end it once and for all, one way or the other. At the same time, he wondered why they were getting so emotional over something that seemed to have no substance. To Swetha, though, the Rahul she had known in college felt like a completely different person from the one standing before her now as her husband.

Back then, he would apologize for every little thing "**Sorry, sorry**," over and over. Now, even when he knew he was wrong, he wouldn't say a word, not even a token of apology.

Why should I be the one to give in?

Let him learn his lesson, she thought bitterly. On Saturday, her phone rang twice. "Rahul… Rahul…" flashed across her iPhone screen. But for some reason, she couldn't bring herself to answer. She knew that if she did, the conversation would only end in another fight.

The next morning, her new friend Nancy dropped by. "Hey, want to go out somewhere?" she asked cheerfully.

"Where to?" Swetha asked. "Oh, maybe a mall, or the casino.

We could grab a bite outside and chill for a bit," Nancy suggested. Swetha wasn't really in the mood, but she thought maybe going out might help clear her head.

Nancy was a local girl, born and brought up here. Her father had moved to California when she was a

child, so she'd studied here all the way from nursery school. Having grown up entirely in America, Nancy's life was shaped by its culture. To her, going to a casino was nothing unusual; it was just another way to spend the weekend. Swetha, on the other hand, knew very little about casinos. Her only impressions came from a few English movies she had seen. The casino they visited was located on the outskirts of the city. Around the world, the most famous casinos are in Las Vegas, the glittering heart of America's gaming world. But here in Cincinnati, the place was smaller—more modest, yet lively in its own way.

For Swetha, it was a completely new experience. In India, gambling was banned, and in many communities, it was considered a vice—something to be avoided, even condemned.

But in America, you must find out for yourself what is good and what is bad. We are not responsible for that — this is the American government. Here, there is freedom for everything. Who had ever escaped the pull of money? The allure was universal, irresistible. Especially in America, where a single dollar could turn into a hundred in the span of a heartbeat.

Yet Swetha couldn't help wondering—what separated the dignity of hard-earned money from the glitter of luck?

What meaning was there in wealth that came without effort?

What kind of legacy could be built on chance? "Why should anyone lose money like this?"

Nancy only shrugged.

"Money is money, sweetheart. It doesn't ask how you got it." Swetha shook her head. Nancy continued.. If God wants to give me money, He can give it anyway.

But even then, I suppose I have to buy the lottery ticket first." Both laughed. "Exactly! Even miracles need a little participation." Swetha's expression softened, though her voice remained firm.

Nancy said. "As far as I'm concerned, casinos are harmless fun. A little thrill, a little entertainment. Nothing more." Their words drifted into the warm room, part teasing, part thoughtful, each woman rooted in her own truth—yet connected by the gentle ease of friendship.

"If you think about it," she continued, "the share market and mutual funds we invest in every day are also a kind of gambling, aren't they? How come only they are seen as respectable ways of earning? Many people have lost all their wealth — even their lives — through those, too."

"If there had been no gambling, the Mahabharata itself wouldn't have happened!

Life itself is a gamble, isn't it?" Nancy didn't seem to stop talking.

Swetha felt there was no point in arguing with her anymore. Nancy took fifty dollars from her elegant Coach vanity bag and began to play. Swetha stood watching everything that was happening around her. For some reason, her heart refused to accept that atmosphere.

She felt she should have spoken to Rahul on the phone. Maybe she shouldn't have cut the call that came yesterday morning. Turning to Nancy, she said, "Come, let's go… It's enough."

Nancy had come to study alone after separating from her husband over a small misunderstanding. And what was that misunderstanding? At home, she believed every household chore should be shared equally. When her husband refused, their marriage came to an end. Even Swetha felt that what Nancy did was right.

After returning to the hostel room, Swetha tried calling Rahul. The phone kept ringing, but there was no response from the other side. She wondered if it was a network issue — or perhaps he simply didn't want to answer. Moments later, Nancy breezed into the room with her usual spark of mischief and freedom. Without hesitation, she uploaded their photo in Facebook and Instagram. — the two of them standing beneath the glowing lights of the casino — and captioned, "**Yes, we won!**" She tagged Swetha, of course, laughing as she hit post, oblivious to how far a single picture could travel, or how deeply it could cut.

Miles away, Rahul, scrolling through Facebook to fill the lonely minutes, felt his heart jolt. There she was — Swetha — standing confidently at the doorway of a casino, her smile bright, her posture carefree... as if the distance between them didn't ache, as if she wasn't missing him the way he had been missing her. A sharp, unexpected sting pierced through him.

What kind of woman is she? he wondered, hurt threading into his thoughts before he could stop it. Life had strange ways of testing the innocent. Swetha had done nothing to deserve his doubts. Rahul knew that — or at least, a gentler part of him did. But the image on the screen, taken so casually, posted so publicly, settled into his heart like a small wound he didn't know how to name. That night, he lay on his bed staring at the ceiling, the glow of the photo still imprinted somewhere deep inside him — and sleep came only as a troubled, uncertain guest.

At 2:00 a.m., his phone rang. It was his father. The news hit like lightning — his mother had passed away. Rahul couldn't process it. How could he get to Chennai immediately from Ahmedabad? Were there any flight tickets available? As he was still thinking, tears began to pour from his eyes. His roommate, Joe, rushed in, booked his ticket, arranged a taxi to the airport, and helped him get on board. Throughout the journey, his mind was filled only with the memories he had shared with his mother.

A mother — the very home of love. He remembered the day he had written his IIT entrance exam and was waiting for the results. The constant support that she rendered stirred his memory. In U.S., Swetha was looking at Rahul's photo with her which they took in Ooty. From early morning onward, no matter how tirelessly she buried herself in her books, no matter how fiercely she fought to remain among the top five students in her class, Swetha found her thoughts drifting back to Rahul. He appeared in her mind with a quiet persistence — a shadow she could neither chase away nor fully embrace.

And yet, with every passing day, her hurt grew sharper, like a wound that refused to close. Why does he never try to understand me? she wondered, anger flickering just beneath her sadness. For the first time, a dangerous, unsettling question whispered through her heart: Had she been too quick in choosing him as her partner for life? The doubt burned inside her —

small at first, then spreading, like a flame catching dry leaves. And just when she was struggling to steady herself, life — as it often does — added a little more fuel to the fire. That evening, Nancy invited her to a party.

She said her close friend Rashna invited both of them for the evening. "I don't feel like going," Swetha murmured. "I have other work." But Nancy, warm and irresistible in her insistence, clasped her hand. "Oh, come on! You must come. Everyone there is wonderful. Trust me — you'll enjoy it." With no graceful way to refuse, Swetha finally agreed. As she dressed, a wave of guilt washed through her.

On the other side, Rahul was mourning his mother, surrounded by grief and rituals and memories… and she, his wife, was stepping out to a party. The unfairness of it stung her deeply. But what choice did she have?

Thousands of miles separated them. No embrace, no whispered comfort, no shared silence was possible. Her love could not cross oceans, not tonight. She felt the ache of that truth settle heavy in her chest — a quiet sorrow she carried with her as she stepped out into the evening. With a confused and heavy heart, Swetha stepped into Nancy's car. On the way, Swetha said, "Let's stop by a Costco or Walmart somewhere. I'll just grab a flower bouquet."Rashna's house was about twenty miles away. There was unusually heavy traffic that day — something they didn't usually see on that route. By the time they arrived, they were ten minutes late. In U.S, people were known for their punctuality — everyone usually showed up exactly on time. Rashna's house was located on the outskirts of the town. She was a close friend of Nancy. Like Nancy, she had grown up and studied in America since childhood. About fifteen people had gathered there. All were students from the same university campus, but from different groups. Some were Indians, some were of Indian origin, a few were Americans, and two were from African and Middle East countries. It was a large house, surrounded by a wide stretch of green lawn. Nearly ten round tables were set up, each covered with a red cloth. At one corner, a separate table was arranged with all kinds of alcoholic drinks and varieties of wine, with just one or two options of orange and apple juice. A barman stood nearby, attending to the guests as they arrived.

Everyone went straight to that corner where the drinks were being served. Each held a glass in hand, saying "Cheers!" to one another, barely letting the drink touch their lips, and spoke in fluent American-accented English that seemed to glide off their tongues. Rashna welcomed Swetha and Nancy warmly and led them directly to the group. "Nancy, I know you'll take vodka and tonic water," Rashna said with a grin.

Then, turning to Swetha, she asked,

"What about you? Will you take wine?"

Flustered, Swetha quickly replied, "No, no… just an orange juice for me." In America, such gatherings were quite normal. By 6 p.m., most people would have had dinner, and afterwards, a drink was almost customary — whether one was twenty or sixty. But for Swetha, all of this was new. One after another, people came up to her, introducing themselves politely. "We've heard so much about you from Nancy," they said. "But it's great to finally meet you in person." Among them was a young man — about six feet two inches tall — dressed in black jeans and a white T-shirt. He looked strikingly like the Bollywood actor Hrithik Roshan. As Swetha continued chatting with others, she didn't notice that from across the room, he had been watching her intently the whole time. He finally approached her and said, "Hi, Swetha… I'm Nancy's friend, Simon. You look so beautiful." Though Swetha didn't like the way he said it, she had no choice but to reply politely, "Thank you."

This was the usual discomfort women faced at such parties.

Some men behaved too casually — sometimes even inappropriately. But avoiding it wasn't always possible. So, they smiled it off. Swetha did the same. While studying in Mumbai, even when he was just a friend, Rahul had never once spoken to her in such a way. He never crossed boundaries. Suddenly, Swetha wondered, Why am I comparing Rahul and Simon? As conversations flowed around her, she realized that nearly half the people at the party had separated from their life partners for some reason and were now living alone. Some were single parents raising children on their own.

In today's world, such situations have become common. Even in India, over the last ten years, things like this had become increasingly frequent. A strange thought came over Swetha — perhaps she didn't belong in this crowd at all.

As the English saying goes, she felt like "the odd man out." So, she went straight to the dinner table. A grand feast was laid out — dishes of every kind, both from the land and the sea. In one small corner, a few vegetarian dishes were arranged, marked with a label that read "Vegetarian." There were only a few options — mostly boiled potatoes and some plain cooked vegetables. Rashna came over to her and asked,

"Are you a vegetarian?" Swetha smiled and replied, "I used to eat non-veg, but after coming to America, I gave it up." Rashna laughed lightly. "That's funny! Most people have started eating everything once they come to America, but you stopped? You're different!"

Just then, an American girl named Carolina joined them. "There are so many vegetarians in India, right? What kind are you?" she asked curiously.

"Yes," said Swetha, "there are many types. Some eat eggs but no meat. Others don't even eat eggs — but if the same egg is in a birthday cake, they'll happily enjoy it!"

"Some are vegetarian only at home," she continued with a small grin, "but when they go out, they eat everything. There are all kinds — countless varieties of vegetarians." But Swetha said calmly,

"Still, I believe vegetarian food is healthier for the body — so I stick to it completely." She smiled, adding lightly, "Just a small personal choice," and took a seat at a nearby round table to begin her meal. *But what Swetha didn't know then was how deeply Carolina's personal story would affect her* — how it would quietly begin to push her towards a decision she never imagined making.

Carolina came closer and said warmly, "Nancy and I have been friends for ten years. I already know quite a bit about you." As they chatted, Carolina suddenly said, "It's really hard living with a husband you can't stand, isn't it? Sometimes it's easier just to walk away." And then she began telling her own story — how she had married her college sweetheart, how much she had loved him at first, and how completely he had changed after marriage. She spoke of the constant fights, the years of stress, and how, after three painful years, she had finally filed for divorce — and now felt free and peaceful again. As Carolina shared one incident after another, Swetha's mind grew restless.

A quiet question began to echo inside her:

Are all men really like that?

Will they change after marriage?

Will they only love the body?

Will they forget the soul?

What a foolish stream of thoughts! "My Rahul isn't like that. He truly loves me. I'm the one who should be a little more patient," she told herself. *In every man and woman in this world, there lives a little monkey inside the mind*— a monkey that drives away all good thoughts and keeps bringing back the bad ones again and again.

That monkey existed in Swetha's mind too. And it began doing its job. "What if I just say goodbye to Rahul without a word and start living on my own?" —whispered that monkey from within. The party was coming to an end. People began to leave one by one. Nancy, who had downed six glasses of wine and was half-stumbling, came up to Swetha and said, "Caroline is absolutely right. Think about it, Swetha. You too could be happy like us." Beyond that, there was nothing more to say. What enmity do we have with Rahul? We've never even seen him. What matters to us is your inner happiness. You deserve to be happy in life — that's all we mean, they said.

In the middle of that, Rashna and Simon came over. "Enough of personal talks, buddy," said Simon. Rashna added, "Google and Amazon are hiring now. They give special preference to big Universities like Cincinnati. Why don't you apply?" "Sure, I will," said Swetha, taking her leave. All along the way, she kept thinking that she must call her parents and discuss this matter. India and U.S. Night here… day there. Day here… night there. She tried twice but couldn't reach them.

The next day in class, everyone was talking about staying back in America for another two years after graduation — something about a visa called OPT. Only now did Swetha slowly begin to understand what visas like OPT and H1B actually meant. No one knows when the Government will change Visa rules. In the college campus, all the girls were discussing about applying for jobs.

Meanwhile, in Chennai… The house overflowed with people — a tide of grief that filled every room. Wails rose and fell like waves crashing against the walls, each cry echoing the unbearable truth: Kamala was gone. "Kamala shouldn't have left us so soon! Two daughters still unmarried… what happened so suddenly?" a woman sobbed, clutching another's shoulder for support. Rahul's father krish was sitting in one corner quietly. Krish's younger sister, Prameela, turned toward Rahul, her eyes swollen with tears.

"What exactly happened, Rahul?" she whispered. But Rahul could not form a single word. His world still felt unreal, as though it had shattered overnight and he was standing amidst the pieces. The call had come while he was in Ahmedabad — abrupt, trembling, breaking through the quiet of the evening. "Son… your mother… she's left us," his father had

said, his voice cracking in a way Rahul had never heard before. For a long moment, Rahul had simply held the phone, unable to breathe, unable even to ask how.

Then, his friend had booked the earliest flight he could find, each hour stretching into a lifetime until he finally reached Chennai. "For the past two days, she kept saying she had chest pain," his father explained now, his voice thin with exhaustion. "We took her to

MMS Hospital. They ran tests… admitted her to the ICU. For four hours the doctors tried. But she had a massive heart attack."

He paused, swallowing hard. "After forty… if someone is diagnosed with diabetes or BP, you are forced to monitor closely and then it is possible to manage. But. when it comes without warning…" His voice trailed away into helplessness. People always recommend yearly medical check-ups, yet the middle class avoided them — afraid of expenses.

Most of them are afraid of walking in completely healthy for full checkup and walking out as a patient. And in that hesitation, danger often slipped in silently. A small dizziness mistaken for tiredness…People try to manage with home remedy to avoid additional expenses.

A heart struggling in silence while life rushed on. Kamala had done the same. A lifetime of home remedies. A lifetime of postponing her own care. In developed countries, people ran to hospitals immediately, insurance shielding them from fear. Illnesses were detected early, sometimes even prevented.

But in India, where insurance helped only with major emergencies, families bore the weight of smaller treatments alone. And so, they waited. They hoped. They prayed. Sometimes, the delay cost them everything. Relatives trickled in one by one, each face carrying shock, sorrow, disbelief. Kamala's body had been placed in the freezer box; the rituals would begin soon.

People held Rahul's and Krish's hands tightly, murmuring words meant to console, though nothing could soften the pain pressing against their chests. Rahul, despite his education, his job, his responsibilities, was drowning in guilt.

Did I fail her? Should I have insisted on check-ups? Could I have saved her?

The questions tormented him relentlessly. In all the chaos, his thoughts hadn't reached Swetha. He had already informed her parents. He assumed she must have heard. She'll come, he told himself, though he didn't know how or when.

When Swetha heard the news, shock washed over her. Nothing felt real. She spoke to her father, her voice trembling, and he gently said, *"They won't be able to keep her body until you reach. Come peacefully, child. Don't rush."* But grief has its own rules — unforgiving, and impossible to rewrite.

Sometimes, one decision — even a well-intentioned one — can change the course of two lives forever.

Parents advise out of love, yet their words can unknowingly build walls between two hearts trying to hold on to each other.

No matter the distance or cost, during moments of profound loss, a husband or wife must stand beside their partner. Presence becomes a lifeline — the silent hand that says, I'm here. You're not alone. A single absence at such a time can carve wounds that never fully heal. There must never be a circumstance that keeps you away. If you fail to go... that absence becomes its own tragedy.

At the Cincinnati campus, all the girls gathered to discuss applying for jobs. Like the other students doing their master's in America, Swetha had applied to companies like Google, Amazon and Microsoft. She also attended one Zoom interview with Google. The way that interviewer spoke to her, she knew that they like her. She felt happy as if she got the job.

Next day: When she opened her email that morning, there was a message from Google — she had been selected for the job she'd been interviewed for. She wanted to share the happy news immediately. First, she wanted to tell Rahul, then her parents. She called Rahul's number — there was no answer. Then she called her father. Her parents were overjoyed. Over the past five years in India, it has become common for at least one member of many families to have gone to America. A son or daughter working at Google or Amazon is now something ordinary.

Rahul took charge of the ten-day rites and all the arrangements — whatever people asked to be done, he coordinated and completed properly. Everyone who came kept asking Rahul,

"Where is Swetha? Where is Swetha?"

Someone nearby would quickly respond, "She's coming next week," or "She'll be here tomorrow."

Rahul remained silent. That silence slowly turned into pain. The tenth-day ritual was completed. Rahul approached the priests who had come to conduct the ceremony and said that he would have to return to

Ahmedabad in a week. Among them was a priest dressed in a traditional panchakatcham (Panchakacham is a traditional way of draping a dhoti with five pleats, commonly worn by men for religious ceremonies and auspicious occasions in South India), with sacred ash and thirunamam on his forehead, and a neatly tied kudumi (a traditional tuft of hair left at the back or top of the head, worn by some Hindu men, especially priests, scholars, and those who follow certain spiritual traditions.)

The team leader of the priests, known as Anju Kodi Iyer, said, “Let me explain.” No one knew his real name. He had earned the name Anju Kodi (meaning five crores in Tamil) because he could chant five crores of sacred mantras without missing a single syllable. He began: “There are still some duties left to be done for your mother,” he said. Rahul asked,

“Why do we do all this?”

To which the priest replied:

“When the soul departs from the body, what really happens? And what help can we, the living, offer to that soul?

That’s what I will explain to you now.

There is something called rebirth...”

A lot of information about this is described in the *Garuda Purana*. After the soul departs, what does your athma (soul) or jivathma do?

When will rebirth occur? We perform all these rites and rituals. Is there any value in all of this?

Must we certainly perform these things?

If we do them, will all our duties be completed?

If we don't perform them, what happens? *One important purpose of a human birth is to attain rebirth-free release — to be spared another birth.* A soul's departure may be natural or premature. Our ancestors, through many Vedic inquiries and debate sessions, devised methods to try to preserve the departing soul so it does not undergo rebirth. Every procedure has reasons behind it. Because most people do not know those reasons, they do not widely perform the rites. These practices are intended so that, when a soul is freed from the body, it will not take rebirth but instead attain Kailash. Much of this is elaborated in the *Garuda Purana.*

We all agree on one fundamental truth — that every being carries the weight of its own karma, composed of paapam (sins) and punya (virtues). Karma is broadly classified into two types: Prarabdha Karma and Sanchita Karma. Prarabdha Karma refers to the accumulated actions carried forward through many births, the inherited destiny that manifests in this lifetime. Sanchita Karma, on the other hand, comprises the deeds of the present birth, the merits and demerits acquired through one's current actions. Depending on the excess balance of these karmas, a soul attains either moksha (liberation - *Moksham* is the state where the soul becomes free, pure, and one with the divine, no longer bound by *karma* or earthly suffering.) or *naragha* (temporary suffering), after which it returns to this world to continue the cycle of births and deaths.

Our duty, therefore, is to assist the departed soul in its journey toward liberation — to help it sever the cycle of rebirth. After death, the soul is said to remain in transition. Immediately after the cremation of the mortal remains, a series of rites must be performed over ten days. On the 13th day, a sacred homa (fire ritual) is offered to Yama, the Lord of Death. There exist many higher realms (lokas) where souls that have transcended rebirth may dwell. Among these, Kashi (Varanasi in state of Uttar Pradesh India) is regarded as the holiest, and within Kashi, Manikarnika Ghat is considered the most exalted site.

While he was describing these sacred truths, a sudden call came for Rahul from the office — *an urgent meeting*. Though physical presence was not required, he was instructed to join via Zoom without delay. Rahul left midway through his quest to understand the reasons behind the rituals performed for his mother and opened his laptop to log in.

It was Saturday—the day he was supposed to return to Ahmedabad after completing the sixteen-day rites. The house was silent. How could he leave his father and two younger sisters alone? Yet, he had no choice. The wedding loans were still unpaid, and now the funeral expenses had added to the burden. He had to earn and stand on his own.

They say that *with time—and with a little salt and spice stirred into one's days—grief softens its sharpest edges.* But for Rahul, nothing had dulled.

Not a memory, not an ache. His mother's absence clung to him with the heaviness of a monsoon sky that refused to break into rain. More than once, he found himself wondering whether he should leave Ahmedabad altogether. Perhaps return to Chennai, to the streets that still carried echoes of her footsteps, to the family that felt suddenly fragile without her.

But duties, responsibilities, and the quiet expectations of the world held him where he was. After days of comforting his father and sisters with the strength he did not feel inside, Rahul finally boarded a flight back to Ahmedabad. Stepping once again through the glass doors of the cybersecurity firm where he worked, One by one, colleagues paused, their voices low with sympathy. Amanda, the poised and always-composed secretary to General Manager Harish Mehta, walked up to him and touched his arm gently. "Boss wanted to see you," she said.

Rahul knocked on the cabin door and entered. Mr. Mehta rose from his chair, his expression unusually warm. "I'm very sorry for your loss, Rahul," he said softly. After a moment, he added,

"There's something important we've been meaning to tell you."

Rahul stood quietly. "We're opening a new branch in Chennai," Mehta said. "And we've decided that you should head it. You will take charge as General Manager – Operations."

For a moment, Rahul simply stared at him. It felt unreal — as though life, *after taking something so precious away, was suddenly placing an unexpected gift in his hands.* Mr. Mehta continued,

"We are also planning to open a branch in California soon. Once you gain experience running Chennai, you'll be transferred there. Company visa. Immediate relocation. Your family will be taken care of too." California.

A future he had never dared imagine. Rahul felt gratitude rise in his chest so fast it almost choked him. He nodded, afraid his voice would betray the storm of emotions he carried. He hoped they would not misinterpret his silence — it wasn't indifference, only a heart too overwhelmed to speak. He left the cabin with a strange mixture of heaviness and hope. He had no way of knowing that the decision he made that afternoon — one made in a haze of grief and longing — would change the entire direction of his life. Once the formalities were completed, Rahul began preparing to move back to Chennai. And beneath everything — the sorrow, the relief, the unexpected fortune — lay the simplest of his desires.

He wanted to share this happy news to Swetha. She needed to know. He hesitated for a moment, wondering if he should. Yet, his heart refused to remain silent. No matter how strained a relationship becomes, when good or bad news arrives, the first person one instinctively wishes to share it with is a spouse. Swetha didn't answer the call. So, he sent her a message.

Two double ticks appeared, a sign that the message had been delivered. But she didn't reply. He couldn't even tell if she had read it.

Rahul soon settled back into life in Chennai. Every morning, he would wake up early, get ready, and head to the IT office located in Temple Tower, Nandanam, the heart of the city. It was a Monday morning. He had an important meeting at 10 a.m., so he left home by 8 a.m.

Although the company had provided him with a car, in a city like Chennai, driving on one's own could still be quite a challenge. According to Rahul, driving in Chennai was far more difficult than driving in Mumbai where he studied. Vehicles seemed to appear from every direction, and even a small mistake on the road could provoke instant anger from others. There was a distinct difference between the people who drove—or even just walked—on the streets of Mumbai and those in Chennai.

Why is everyone here in Chennai are so easily irritated? Perhaps, he thought, it was because of the city's harsh climate. When one's body is constantly drenched in sweat, it's hard not to lose patience. That's the main difference between cooler regions and scorching cities: while one offers pleasant greenery and a gentle climate, the other blazes under relentless heat.

People living in colder regions, he thought, rarely lose their temper. Their minds remain calm and composed.

But what could anyone do?

For the sake of livelihood, people from every corner of Tamil Nadu had moved to Chennai. Even if they tried their best to control their temper, the strain of the city sometimes forced it to surface.

By the time Rahul entered the office, it was already 9:30 a.m. The meeting with the American client was scheduled for 10:00 sharp.

As he walked past the glass cubicles, he told his secretary to call Project Manager Robin and the team—Atheera, Girish, and John Mathews—into his cabin, along with the complete set of documents for the presentation. Within minutes, the room was filled. Laptops open, cables coiled on the table, screens lighting up as everyone prepared for the POC (proof of concept demonstration) through Microsoft Teams. The pressure in the air was unmistakable.

The client expected perfection. One frozen screen, one faulty button, one loading delay — and months of work could collapse like a house of cards. Rahul scanned the room. "Is everything ready?" he asked, calm on the surface, though his heartbeat drummed with urgency. Just then, his phone lit up. Swetha on the other side. On any normal day, Rahul rarely answered calls during work. Years of corporate conditioning had taught him that discipline meant silence — phones off, distractions dismissed, attention sharp as a blade. He didn't even think. His thumb moved on instinct. The call vanished from the screen. He didn't realize that, thousands of miles away, Swetha would see that small action as something far bigger.

As rejection. As distance. As indifference.

Rahul, already buried in work, forgot the call almost instantly. He turned back to Robin. "Start the demo." Two screens performed flawlessly. The AI-based mobile application flowed smoothly — intuitive, responsive, promising.

But on the third screen, the loading symbol spun endlessly… then froze. A cold silence settled over the room. Rahul's jaw tightened. "What is this?" he asked, voice clipped. Robin leaned forward, sweating. "Sir… it's a small network issue. We'll fix it in two minutes." Rahul closed his eyes for a moment, steadying himself. Software is software, he reminded himself. There will always be defects. Always something waiting to go wrong. But not today. Not with an American client who believed politeness was diplomacy and diplomacy was rejection.

Rahul knew their language too well — If they say, "Very nice, thank you very much for your time. We'll get back to you," it was a polite way of saying the project was lost.

He stood behind Robin, watching every move, every correction on the screen, knowing exactly what was at stake — his reputation, his team's effort, the company's trust, and the future he was trying so hard to rebuild. And yet, somewhere in the background of his mind… there was Swetha's unanswered call, ringing in a corner of his heart he didn't have time to acknowledge.

Rahul knew very well that the software bug issue couldn't be fixed in just two minutes. Without wasting a second, he called the company's CIO, Mr.

Brian Wilkie, in the U.S. and requested a three-hour extension.

By sheer luck, Brian replied, "I have another meeting to attend. Let's reschedule this demo for the same time tomorrow." That single sentence felt like a lifeline. A full day meant they could fix everything and deliver a perfect demonstration. After everyone from the project team left, Rahul asked Robin to stay back.

He looked at him intently and said, "I had a lot of faith in you, Robin. What happened? Why didn't you test it properly before the demo?" For the past two days, I've been going through a personal problem. I just couldn't concentrate on work," said Robin quietly. Usually, Rahul never entertained discussions about anyone's personal life in the office. But this time, something made him pause. Against his own habit, he asked, Robin hesitated at the door, his hand lingering on the frame as though gathering the courage to speak. "What's the problem, Robin?" Rahul asked softly. Robin lifted his face, and for a moment he looked far younger than he was — vulnerable, exhausted, almost fragile.

Robin looked straight into Rahul's eyes. Tiny droplets formed at the corners of his lashes as he began to speak. "My wife has decided to leave me," he whispered, his voice cracking on the last word. "We have a one-year-old child. I've begged her to talk things through… but she won't listen anymore. I… don't know how to hold the pieces together." He let out a breath that sounded like it had been trapped inside him for months. "We fell in love," he said, staring at the floor as though their memories were scattered there. "We got married against all odds. For a while we were happy , peacefully happy. But for the past two years… it's been nothing but storms. Every word I speak seems to ignite her anger. Her parents blame me. Mine blame her." He rubbed his temples, as though trying to ease a pain far deeper than a headache. "I feel trapped, sir. Pulled apart by both families. We both work full-time in IT. When I try to help with chores, my parents are furious."

My parents often say that… 'We raised you like a king… and now you're washing dishes?'" Then he sighed. "And my wife says, 'I was raised like a queen. Why should I be the only one doing the housework?'" He tried to smile, but it broke halfway. "She earns twenty thousand more than me. And still my parents believe she must handle every chore alone. Her parents say she deserves rest too. And between all this… we've forgotten how to breathe." Rahul listened quietly, his heart tightening a little. Even Swetha and I argue every day, he thought. Every couple carries their own burdens. Every home has its shadows "Why don't you hire help?" Rahul asked gently. He knew even as he spoke that the answer wouldn't be simple. Robin shook his head. "My parents are orthodox. From a small village. They believe a home should be run only by the family. No maids. No compromise. And that's where every fight begins." Silence settled between them — the heavy kind that carries too much truth. If they separate in anger, will life become easier? Rahul wondered.

Or will it only grow emptier… colder… lonelier? He placed a comforting hand on Robin's shoulder. "Focus on your work for now," Rahul said gently, his voice warm but steady. "Everything else… somehow, someday… will find its way."

As they were talking, two other project members, Atheera and Girish, walked in. "All the testing is complete, sir", they said. "Everything's working perfectly." They showed the demo to Rahul. The demo had turned out really well. This will do, Rahul thought. If we present this properly and explain it clearly to the American company's team, the project will surely be ours. According to the plan, once the UAT (User Acceptance Test) was completed at their San Francisco branch and approved by their technical team, the rollout would proceed across 300 locations. The next day, as expected, the project demo took place. After the presentation, everyone attending the meeting from the American company applauded enthusiastically.

"**Excellent!** This is exactly what we were looking for," they said. Soon after, a purchase order worth three million dollars arrived at the Ahmedabad head office.

From there, Rahul's boss called him in for a meeting. "**Congratulations**… you did it!" Rahul's boss looked at him with unmistakable pride, the kind a mentor feels when a student finally steps into his own light.

He entrusted Rahul with the responsibility of hiring an entire team for the new project, asking him to build it from the ground up with talent from Chennai itself. From that moment, Rahul's days became a whirlwind of interviews, tight deadlines, and impossible expectations — the kind he somehow kept meeting with calm determination. Slowly, almost quietly, the Chennai branch began earning a reputation among their American clients.

Number of staff reached from hundred to five hundred plus. And at the heart of it all was Rahul — steady, dependable, brilliant in the way only someone who had endured loss and rebuilt himself could be. Everyone in the office admired him; some even adored him. Meanwhile, far away in Ahmedabad, the head office was busy shaping their next dream — a new branch in California. And they wanted Rahul to lead it. It felt unreal. A few months ago, life had felt unbearably heavy. But now, everything seemed to be aligning in a way he hadn't dared to imagine. When two people truly understand each other, Rahul often thought, marriage becomes the holiest of bonds. Not wealth, not power, not even becoming the CEO of a global IT firm could match the peace that comes from a loyal partnership. It was a truth he believed in with all his heart — and one he longed to experience. That evening, he returned home with a happiness he hadn't felt in years.

He wanted to tell his father and sisters everything — that their struggles would soon end, that he would one day rise to become a cybersecurity expert, perhaps even the CEO – Chief Executive Officer of his company. And all of it… in California. Not everyone could become a Sundar Pichai; destiny chose a few rare souls for heights like that. But Rahul felt, for the first time, that he was at least walking toward something extraordinary. He imagined himself at international gatherings where CEOs from across the world sat together — no big company, no small company, no comparisons.

A CEO is a CEO. And he could be one of them very soon. A glow of pride spread through him, warm and freeing. The inferiority complex that had shadowed him for so many years had, at last, begun to dissolve. Confidence settled into the space it left behind. But destiny rarely moves in straight lines. But that night was anything but pleasant.

Late that night, as Rahul was preparing to sleep, the glow of his phone lit up the dim room. It was an email from Swetha. With a calmness that felt almost cruel, she had written a long message. But the six devastating words: "***We can no longer live together." He glanced at the screen — and froze.*** Below it, in firm, final sentences, she stated her decision to seek a divorce. She had even copied her family's lawyer on the email, as if to seal the formality of it, as if their marriage had already ended. Rahul felt the ground slip beneath him. His breath came slow and heavy, as though he had been struck. No matter how angry she had been, this… this was something he never expected. Once again, she had been the one to act first, the one to make decisions that should have belonged to both of them. A storm rose inside him — anger on one side, a hollow ache on the other.

How could he tell his father and sisters?

What sin had he committed that he deserved this?

He wondered, with a quiet desperation, whether their marriage might have survived if they had only tried a little harder… adjusted a little more.

But then, another thought pushed through the chaos. Enough. Enough of hurting. Enough of trying alone. Sometimes it was better to live alone — or with someone who cared — than to remain bound to a person who no longer understood you, who no longer even tried. She had made the choices, yes. But the punishment sat on both their shoulders. He stared at the blinking cursor, his emotions spilling faster than reason could catch them. In a sudden wave of fury, he began typing — listing her faults one by one, the resentments he had swallowed for months. And at the end of it, he typed: *"I'm equally happy about the separation. Let's proceed with the arrangements immediately."* The words burned on the screen, sharp and unkind. But anger has a way of blinding a man's wisdom, silencing the voice that asks him to wait… to breathe. Rahul kept typing.

If you wish to live with me, then you must move to Chennai.

We should start a family soon.

You should take good care of my father and sisters. Same I will do for your parents.

If you agree to this, we can continue our life together. If not, let's part ways peacefully." He read the lines again — harsh, wounded, demanding.

There was a moment, a tiny moment, when he hesitated. When the part of him that still loved her asked him to stop. But frustration, heartbreak, and anger twisted together inside him — and his finger pressed **Send** button before he even realized it.

It was all done.

He was looking at the options of calling the mail back But, Swetha already received in her inbox. This time, the time difference between India and U.S. worked against him. The mail has gone.... Irreversible. Out of his hands now. Rahul leaned back, his chest tightening with a dull exhaustion. "Why is it," he wondered bitterly, "that I am always the one who must suffer so much?"

But life, he knew, was never a bed of roses for anyone. Joy and sorrow comes in alternating tides, each with its own lessons, its own wounds. And now, another tide had come for him. The day came that

Swetha had to travel back to India. She sent her itenary to her parents and one copy to Rahul. Swetha had arrived in Pune — carrying both a heavy heart from the past two months of turmoil and new dreams of beginning a life on her own. The plane touched down at Pune Airport. Usually, passengers arriving from the United States land in Mumbai first. But this time, Swetha had taken a different route — flying from Chicago to Dubai via Emirates, waiting there for two hours, and then continuing to Dubai - Pune. The exhaustion from the long journey tugged at her body, while the quiet satisfaction of her academic success soothed her mind. Yet, through it all, thoughts of Rahul lingered like an unshakable echo. Before leaving the U.S., she had told her father, "Please, none of you come to the airport. I'll just take a prepaid taxi from inside." But the real reason behind her request was something else — a faint hope that perhaps Rahul might come to receive her.

Her eyes searched for him in the crowd at the airport.

Dozens of people stood outside the arrival gates. As passengers streamed out, friends and relatives waved eagerly, ran forward to hug them, and shared their joy in warm embraces. Rahul hadn't spoken to her. He probably hadn't even read her message saying she was coming to India.

And above all, after the email about the divorce and the curt reply he had sent in anger, expecting him to come and take her home was pure foolishness. Even when her mind questioned, "Are you sure about this?" her heart whispered, "He'll come… everything will be fine." Standing in line, she stepped into the taxi she had booked. Handing the driver the prepaid receipt, she checked quickly — the two suitcases, the laptop bag, and her wallet containing her passport and boarding pass — all were safe. Swetha was thanking her dad for teaching these small things for a smooth travel.

It would take at least an hour and a half to reach home through this traffic. How different the roads were in America, vehicles moved quietly, almost respectfully, without a single honk. But here, it was as though every driver felt personally responsible for reminding the world that his horn worked perfectly. She leaned back in her seat and closed her eyes.

Slowly, her thoughts drifted, slipping into the warm, familiar corridors of memory… back to the days leading up to the wedding. Rahul had flown to Chennai a week before her. And when Swetha arrived the following week, the first thing she saw through the sliding airport doors was him—standing outside the barrier, searching every face with an urgency that made her heart flutter. His gaze swept the crowd again and again, hope lighting up each time someone emerged. Was that her?

Half an hour later, when she finally stepped out, Rahul spotted her in an instant. He walked straight toward her, gently took the bag from her hand, and wrapped her in a warm embrace—one that spoke more than words ever could. In that single hug, she felt the certainty of his love. Anticipating she might have come with several bags, Rahul had arranged a Toyota Innova travel car in advance. They settled into the backseat.

The driver turned and asked respectfully, "Rahul sir, straight home?" "No… not home yet. First, we need to stop at VR Mall in Anna Nagar," Rahul said, his eyes still lingering on Swetha with unmistakable affection. "We'll go there first."

The drive was calm, the air between them filled with an unspoken joy. At the mall's underground parking, the vehicle stopped, and the driver offered to wait. Rahul and Swetha made their way up the escalators to the third floor. "Look at this," Rahul said gently. "You must be hungry. There's a place called Kailash Parbat—your favorite dish is there."

Swetha hadn't even realized how hungry she was until that moment. Rahul returned soon with Chole Battura, the exact thing she loved. The moment she tasted it, warmth spread through her—his thoughtfulness, his attention to the smallest details of her happiness, meant more than he knew. Saying I love you ten times a day is one kind of affection. But the subtle act of remembering what one's partner loves—and quietly offering it—was a deeper, more intimate language of the heart.

Swetha felt her chest fill with emotion. She told herself, with a certainty that made her eyes sting, *I chose the right man.* This love will last my whole life. After the meal, Rahul walked to the Madras Coffee counter and said, "one filter coffee and one Masala Chai… please."

The serving lady on the other side asked " Sir.. do you want me to add Sugar…" Rahul said.. No need…. Swetha likes strong Coffee without sugar, she started taking coffee after meeting Rahul and he did not know when he started liking Tea.. By the time Swetha came near to the counter and said "One is enough," Swetha said softly. "Let's share."

Rahul smiled, a smile that warmed her more than the coffee ever could. "From now on," he said gently, "everything in life will be shared equally." The simple statement carried the weight of a promise. And Swetha felt it settle into her heart. Rahul cancelled the Tea and took one cup of coffee. They sipped the coffee looking at each other eyes.

After finishing their coffee on the escalator and descending to the lower floor, Swetha placed her foot on the same step where Rahul had set his. Gradually, she balanced herself, took his hand, and stood beside him on the next step.

"The bond of '**I for you, you for me**' brings me such happiness," she thought.

With hearts brimming with joy, they entered the branded stores in the mall one by one. In the Louis Vuitton store, a handbag priced at ₹2,00,000 caught their eye.

The attendant asked, "Would you like to take this one? "Rahul turned to Swetha and said, "Pick the handbag you like." She smiled and asked about the budget.

Rahul replied, "There is no budget. Choose whatever you like." Swetha selected a grey-colored handbag from the next floor, branded Lavi Luxé, priced at ₹5,400.

For the first time, Rahul felt immense joy in gifting something that his girl truly desired. No matter the financial effort involved, if a husband buys something that his wife truly desires, for the next few minutes, there is a quiet dignity and grace in her presence. Rahul understood this instinctively. And that is exactly how he acted. By the time they reached home, it was already 4:00 p.m.

At the threshold, his father asked.

"Why you took so long ?" Due to Traffic ? Rahul replied, "The flight was very late." Sometimes, these small, harmless little excuses (small lies) spoken to elders are forgiven. There is no need to burden them with the truth and make both them and ourselves uneasy.

Suddenly, Swetha's car came to a stop. Her eyes widened. She woke up from that day dream..

She realized that there is no Rahul next to her. She had finally reached home. Her parents were standing outside, waiting. She wondered, Will we ever find again that hill of happiness we once visited in our dreams? And what must we do to reach it? She remembered reading somewhere that change comes only when we learn to accept certain truths in life. That when we transform ourselves, our lives too begin to transform. *Love,* she had read, is something profoundly deep— it does not thrive on the need to conquer one another, nor does it survive on expectations. Swetha recalled reading something like the above in one of the Nora Roberts novel that she read when she was in college. As soon as she entered the house and saw her parents, a small sense of calm settled within her. At the same time, there was a quiet apprehension about what her life would hold next. Until late at night, she spoke with her father about the American university and her Google interview. She did not mention Rahul, nor did she speak of the decision regarding her marital life.

Her father said gently, "You must be tired. Go and rest. We can talk in the morning." The next morning, she and her father sat on the balcony, coffee in hand. The cool breeze brushed past them. Even though the view from the hostel balcony in America had been picturesque, today, sitting here in India, breathing in the fresh local air with her parents brought a quiet peace to her heart. Perhaps this is what they call the "breath of independence." Her father spoke slowly, his voice gentle but weighted with concern. "Swetha, tell me… what troubles you?

What is happening between you and Rahul?"
He searched her face, trying to read the ache she had been hiding. "You both married out of love," he reminded her softly. "We have never forced anything on you." Swetha looked away, her throat tightening. "I… I can't explain it," she said finally, her voice barely above a whisper. "The Rahul I imagined… the Rahul I loved… he feels different now. And the man I see today—he is not the person I thought I was building a life with." She paused, fighting back the swirl of emotions rising inside her. "I cannot settle in Chennai just because he wants me to. He has his dreams, his path… but for that I cannot leave everything behind and dress each day in the way he expects. To me, a husband and wife are equal. But what he wants is a conventional Indian wife—someone who says 'Yes' to everything he decides, who shapes her whole world around his wishes, who runs the house and raises the children exactly as he imagines."

She shook her head slowly. "That isn't me. I cannot live as a 'Yes, boss' wife." Her father listened without interrupting, absorbing every word, his eyes soft with a father's compassion. "Be patient, Swetha," he said at last, his voice steady and reassuring. "Sometimes love finds its way, even through confusion. Everything will work out. Give it a little time." For the first time, Swetha realized that listening to her words was different for her father. He was giving guidance without dismissing her feelings. She had always thought he would approve of whatever she did, but today he was different—he was showing her, without saying it outright, where she might be mistaken.

As they continued talking, Ria her favorite kid from the neighboring house arrived. Seeing her after a long time, the little girl hugged her tightly. Swetha handed her the small toys and chocolates she had brought from America. But Ria's mother, Kinjal, who had hurried over, gently stopped her. "No, Swetha. We've stopped giving chocolates to Ria. It's not a good habit," she said, picking up the child and taking her back to her house.

Swetha's mother, observing everything closely, remarked, "A child from the neighboring house is just another child. But, You should have one of your own. Only then can you truly celebrate your rights over your child." Swetha understood the wisdom in her mother's words.

Curiously, she asked her mother, "How did you manage to adjust to everything with Dad? How do you wear the clothes he likes? Is your mother-in-law very kind?" Swetha's mother replied, "My mother-in-law never asked me to do anything for her sake. She simply said, 'Wear the clothes your husband likes.' She gave me complete freedom." Swetha reflected on this and thought,

"What freedom can there really be when a wife only wears what her husband likes?" She didn't quite understand it yet.

This, she realized, was what people referred to as the "generation gap."

On the other side in Chennai…

In their modest Ashok Nagar home in Chennai, after his mother had left, Rahul sat down for the first time in years to share a meal alone with his father. The silence between them felt unfamiliar, almost fragile. His father broke it gently. "So… any news from Swetha?" Rahul didn't look up. "Yes. We're going to part ways." There was no shock on his father's face, no dramatic reaction. Just a quiet nod. "Alright," he said softly. "Eat first. We'll talk once you finish." After the meal, father and son sat across from each other in the small sitting room sofa—two adults in a conversation that life had delayed for far too long. Since childhood, Rahul had turned to his mother for everything: school troubles, bruised knees, heartbreaks, uncertainties. She had always been his first confidante.

But today was different. Today, his mother wasn't here. And in her place, his father sat quietly, patiently, waiting. "I don't feel respected," Rahul began, the words heavy but honest about Swetha. “She won’t come to Chennai. She wants to work only in America. She doesn’t want to have a child. There are… so many problems like this, every day.” His father listened, then spoke in a slow, measured voice. “These kinds of problems exist in every marriage, Rahul.

There is no such thing as a perfect couple. No two people agree on everything.”

He paused, letting the words settle. “Even a daughter-in-law who never visited when her mother-in-law passed away…

What sort of daughter-in-law she is…. Rahul said…. His father was quiet … Relationships don’t disappear because of shortcomings. You chose her. What seemed beautiful to you then may seem different now—not because she changed, but because your perspective has. Rahul looked at him, surprised by the clarity and calm with which his father spoke. “That is Swetha,” his father continued. The same self-confidence, the same certainty, the same determination she had before the wedding. That day, all of it felt admirable. Today, it feels different. He looked directly into Rahul’s eyes.

“Do you know why?” Rahul waited.

“Because then, it was before the wedding…

and now, it is after the wedding.”

The words struck deep in the quiet room. “Shift your perspective just a little,” his father said gently. “You will see her change too—perhaps in ways you like, perhaps in ways you never expected.” Rahul sat back, absorbing every word.

The father he had always assumed knew less than his mother… was speaking with a wisdom he had never heard before. For the first time, Rahul paused—truly paused—to think about what his father had said. Unbeknownst to Rahul, Krish had already spoken to Swetha's father and quietly arranged for her trip to Chennai. And so, the next morning at exactly eight, a Uber car pulled up at the entrance of the house. Swetha stepped out with her parents, looking both unsure and determined, like a woman ready to face whatever waited on the other side of the door. Rahul stood inside, uncertain how to welcome her after everything that had passed between them. Before he could take a step, his sister Meena rushed forward, took Swetha gently by the hands, and guided her inside with the warmth of a sister who had been waiting for this moment. In the living room, Kamala's framed photograph hung on the wall, draped with a garland of fresh roses. Swetha walked straight to it. She closed her eyes in silent prayer, touched the photo with trembling fingertips, and pressed it to her forehead in a gesture of deep respect and remorse. From a distance, Rahul watched her. He looked at his mother's face in the photograph, and in those soft, familiar eyes, he felt something like a blessing—quiet, wordless, and perfectly timed. Everything, somehow, was falling slowly into place. Swetha's father turned to Rahul.

"We'll go out for a while… up to the Vadapalani Murugan temple. You and Swetha should have some time together. You both can go out for lunch.. We may not be able to join." Rahul nodded, understanding exactly what he meant.

By one o'clock, he was wondering where to take her for lunch. He knew her favorites by heart—small details he treasured more than he admitted. She loved BBQ Nation. It wasn't grand or elaborate, but it was hers, and that was enough. They sat in a quiet corner of the restaurant, the silence between them tender rather than heavy. Swetha looked at him with eyes that carried longing, regret, and something even deeper. "What will you have?" he asked gently. "**Anything,**" she said.

He smiled for the first time in days. "There's no dish called '**Anything.**'" It took her back to their early days in Mumbai—their first little dates, their quiet laughter—and she couldn't help but smile. Same question from him.. same answer.. " ***Anything*** .." that word meant everything today; taking them back to the day when they first went out together. Her voice trembled slightly as she spoke. "I'm really sorry for not coming when your mother passed. I should have been with you. You were alone… and I wasn't there. I had exams the next week, and with the visa stamping with these new rules and delays in appointments, I was afraid I wouldn't be able to return." For the first time, Rahul truly saw the fear behind her decision—the helplessness she had tried so hard to hide. "It's alright," he said softly. "My mother will understand. She always did. And we don't have to answer to anyone else." Swetha took a breath. "I got a job offer from Google." He looked up sharply.

"But I'm not taking it," she continued. "I want to be here with you… in Chennai. I'll find a job here." It felt like the first ball of a cricket match, hit beautifully for **four**—effortless, relieving, full of promise.

Rahul shook his head gently. "You don't have to give anything up. My company is sending me to California. I'll have to join in two months." Just like that, two impossibilities dissolved into possibilities. And then, out of nowhere, as if carried on a sudden wave of hope, she said quietly, "We can have a child soon." Because of that incident in Pune—with their neighbor Kinjal's little daughter Ria—something inside Swetha had shifted quietly, almost imperceptibly, but deeply enough to change the way she looked at her own future. She felt firmly what her mother said was true that she should have her own child.

Rahul felt a sudden, joyful shock. A child. A life together. A future. It seemed as if the second ball of the innings is a **big sixer**. All the things he had convinced himself would never happen seemed to be falling gently back into his hands. "I shouldn't have sent that email listing your faults," he said, his voice catching. "I'm so sorry." He laughed softly. It reminded her of their college days—when he would make a tiny mistake during a project and say "Sorry, sorry" in that same earnest tone, the words tumbling out with genuine sincerity. She felt something warm bloom inside her.

Happiness—simple and unguarded. "And within a year," she added, "the sisters can get married. We must also look after dad properly. A medical check-up every six months, no excuses." Rahul felt a quiet ache in his chest—how had he ever doubted the woman who cared so deeply, so instinctively, for the people he loved?

After lunch, they stepped out together—lighter, calmer, teasing each other like the young couple they once were. And perhaps, like the couple they were finally ready to become again. Swetha had a flight to Pune the next morning, but that night, she and Rahul stayed in the same room where they had spent their early, blissful days of marriage. The room still carried memories—soft laughter, whispered dreams, the warmth of two people learning to belong to each other. In the quiet darkness, Rahul reached for her hand. Slowly, hesitantly. Even as a small voice in his mind told him the moment was fragile, she didn't pull away. Instead, her fingers tightened around his—as though seeking an anchor she had long missed. After so many days, the old feeling returned.

The simple, overwhelming joy of knowing she was made for him, and he for her. For Swetha, the closeness felt natural—like stepping back into a rhythm her heart had always known. She trusted him completely, not because she surrendered herself, but because love had always been their safest place.

A wife who feels no need to prove her superiority, and a husband who expresses his thoughts with clarity—especially to a wife who truly understands him—form the foundation of a successful bond. In such a union, the harmony of mind and body knows no bounds.

That is what happened here. Rahul lying on his bed, wondering they had rushed things, they had blown up small issues that needed discussion, and yet, without her knowing, Swetha rested her head on his chest and began to sleep similar to her honeymoon nights at Ooty. For those two, it felt as if all their troubles had been resolved, and a rare peace settled over them.

The emotional maturity required in a marriage is the ability to forgive the spouse who may have hurt you, and not let that wound resurface when the opportunity arises. Doing so without bringing back what is to be forgotten is a blessing.

That is what strengthens a marital bond. The next morning… Swetha stepped out of the shower wrapped in the soft scent of jasmine. She dressed carefully, choosing a chiffon saree in Rahul's favorite shade of sunshine yellow. With the delicate flowers pinned into her hair, she walked to the framed photograph of Rahul's mother, bowed her head, and offered her silent prayers. Then she turned to his father, Krish, and bent to touch his feet. He placed a gentle hand on her head and said, with the quiet blessing of a man who had seen much in life, "God bless you my child… be happy. Everything will be fine."

A week later, the familiar hum of Chennai Airport wrapped around them. The announcement echoed through the speakers in the distinct Malayalam-accented Tamil of the staff: "Emirates Flight EK 542 to Dubai is now ready for boarding." Swetha and Rahul walked side by side, carry-on bags in hand, laptops slung over their shoulders. Their journey would stretch from Chennai to Dubai, and from there to San Francisco—towards a life they had almost lost, but somehow reclaimed. Just before departure, her phone buzzed. A message from Nancy in the U.S.:
"Heard the good news —how did you two get together?"
Swetha smiled, typed back a simple, "**Plain talking**" , and switched off her phone. Moments later, the Emirates aircraft—one that ferried thousands of travelers each day—lifted smoothly into the sky. And today, among those thousands, it carried Rahul and Swetha too… rising upward, as if carrying with it the blessing of a new beginning, soaring toward a life waiting to be lived happily ever after.

9789372544381